Carnegie Endowment for International Peace
DIVISION OF INTERNATIONAL LAW

AN ESSAY

ON A

CONGRESS OF NATIONS

FOR THE ADJUSTMENT OF INTERNATIONAL DISPUTES
WITHOUT RESORT TO ARMS

BY

WILLIAM LADD

Reprinted from the original edition of 1840
with an introduction

by

JAMES BROWN SCOTT

NEW YORK
OXFORD UNIVERSITY PRESS
AMERICAN BRANCH: 35 WEST 32ND STREET
LONDON, TORONTO, MELBOURNE, AND BOMBAY
HUMPHREY MILFORD
1916

THE QUINN & BODEN CO. PRESS
RAHWAY, N. J.

INTRODUCTION

Our distinguished fellow countryman, Elihu Burritt, known alike as a scholar and a philanthropist, summed up in the following paragraph, written in 1871, the claim to grateful remembrance of his master and friend, William Ladd, whom he delighted to call the apostle of peace and whose *Essay on a Congress of Nations for the Adjustment of International Disputes without Resort to Arms,* originally published in 1840, is here reproduced:

When we consider that such a permanent High Court of Nations [advocated by Mr. Ladd in the Essay] would not only be the noblest and loftiest bar that could be established on earth for the appeal and settlement of all serious questions of difficulty between them, but that such a bar would be a bond of confederation to them, we must recognize the fullness of Mr. Ladd's plan for abolishing war, and establishing permanent and universal peace. He gave to the advocacy and development of this scheme years of indefatigable faith and effort. He enlisted a large number of writers to elaborate it with their best arguments and illustrations. As a stimulus to these efforts, the American Peace Society offered $1,000 as a prize for the best essay on the subject. A considerable number were produced, and submitted to such a jury of award as Wirt, Webster, Story, and Marshall could form. As their excellence was so good and even, the jury could not desire to say which was the best. So, six of them were published in a large volume by the Society, including one written by Mr. Ladd himself, which developed the scheme more completely than any of the rest, and which to this day is accepted as its best exponent and argument. This was the largest and most costly volume ever published on either side of the Atlantic on the subject of peace. As soon as it left the press, Mr. Ladd set himself to the work of distributing copies to the crowned heads and leading men of Christendom with all the glowing zeal and activity which he brought to the cause. And it is the best tribute to his clear judicious mind that the main proposition as he developed it has been pressed upon the consideration of the public mind of

iii

Christendom ever since his day, without amendment, addition, or subtraction. The writer of these introductory notes, who was one of Mr. Ladd's disciples and successors, felt it his duty to present the proposition, pure and simple as his master developed it, at the great Peace Congresses at Brussels, Paris, Frankfort, and London; and to-day it stands before the world, the scheme of William Ladd.*

If this language was true, as it undoubtedly was, thirty years after Mr. Ladd's death, it is equally true at the present day, some forty-four years after Mr. Burritt's tribute, and seventy-four years after the death of William Ladd, when the Congress which he proposed, to agree upon the principles of international law, had been called in 1898 by a " respectable state," to use the words of the *Essay*, and when the Court of Nations which he advocated was approved, in 1907, in the second Conference of the Nations, likewise called by the same respectable state, and when the Court itself can be said to be in the process of formation.

The career of a man whose services have been so highly rated, but not over-rated, by Mr. Burritt, and whose project is being carried out slowly and piecemeal by the Hague Conference, whose possibility he foresaw and whose labors he outlined, deserves to be recorded and to be placed before persons interested in international organization. And yet, like those whose lives are merged in their ideals, there is but little to relate. Mr. Ladd was born in Exeter, New Hampshire, on the 10th day of May, 1778. He fitted for college at the academy of his native town; he entered Harvard College in 1793; and he graduated with the class of 1797. He followed the sea for a number of years, to which he returned after a philanthropic but not altogether successful experience in Florida, but left it permanently upon the outbreak of the War of 1812 with Great Britain. In 1812 he settled at Minot in the State of Maine upon a farm which had belonged to his father. The successful management of his modest inheritance, to which he added from time to time, made him independent, indeed wealthy, and he was therefore able to devote the leisure of the winter season, and to give very considerable sums of money, to causes of a philanthropic nature in which he was inter-

---

* John Hemmenway, *Memoir of William Ladd*, 1872, introductory notes, pp. 14-5.

ested. He died at Portsmouth, New Hampshire, on April 7th, 1841.

In his early years, indeed until 1819, Mr. Ladd is not known to have taken any interest in peace as such, and his connection with the movement was as accidental to him as it was fortunate to the cause of peace. His own account is as follows:

> I had the privilege of witnessing some of the last hours of the Rev. Jesse Appleton, D.D., President of Bowdoin College. In his joyful anticipations of the growing improvement of the world, and the enumeration of the benevolent societies of the day, he gave a prominent place to *Peace Societies;* and this was almost the first time I ever heard of them. The idea then passed over my mind as the day-dream of benevolence; and so every one views the subject, who does not examine it. It is probable that the impressions made at this interview first turned my attention to the subject, but it probably would soon have escaped from me, had not the *Solemn Review* *, which came soon after into my possession, in a very singular way, riveted my attention in such a manner as to make it the principal object of my life to promote the cause of Peace on earth and good-will to man.†

Leaving out of consideration isolated expressions in favor of peace, to be found in the writings of Dr. Franklin, in the letters and state papers of Washington as private citizen and as President, and the negotiation of the Jay Treaty of 1794, which called attention to arbitration and introduced it again into the practice of nations, it may be said that the first attempt to bring the friends of peace together and to combine their efforts in a movement to advance the cause of peace dates from 1809, in which year Mr. David Low Dodge, a high-minded and successful merchant of New York City, published a tract entitled *The Mediator's Kingdom not of this World: but Spiritual*, in which, to quote his own words, he bore " public testimony against the anti-Christian custom of war." Mr. Dodge reports, in his interesting autobiography, that during the ensuing year " more than twenty leading members of evangelical churches

---

* *A Solemn Review of the Custom of War*, a pamphlet by the Rev. Noah Worcester, D.D., published by the American Peace Society in 1814.

† Hemmenway, op. cit., p. 38.

appeared fully to embrace the doctrine of peace on earth and good-will to men, repudiating the spirit and maxims of war." *

Two or three years later he wrote:

> By this time the friends of peace in New York had so much increased, that early in 1812, they deliberated on the expediency of forming a peace society, wholly confined to decided evangelical Christians, with a view to diffuse peace principles in the churches, avoiding all party questions. Our object was not to form a popular society, but to depend, under God, upon individual personal effort, by conversation and circulating essays on the subject; . . .
>
> At this juncture, there was much political excitement and war was threatened against Great Britain, and fearing that our motives would be misapprehended we judged it not wise to form a peace society openly, until the public mind was more tranquil. In the mean time we resolved to be active individually in diffusing information on the subject, and answering the objections of our friends. I was appointed to prepare an essay on the subject, stating and answering objections.†

The result was the preparation and publication, in 1812, of an elaborate tractate entitled *War Inconsistent with the Religion of Jesus Christ*,‡ which expanded and modified the views briefly set forth in the *Mediator's Kingdom*,‡ and which can at this day be taken as an authoritative exposition of the views of those who believe that defensive as well as offensive war is inconsistent with the Christian religion.

A further quotation from the autobiography shows not only Mr. Dodge's interest in the peace movement but the progress it was making. " The friends of peace," he said, " had two or three meetings relative to the organization of a society. In August, 1815, they unanimously formed the New York Peace Society, of between thirty and forty members, probably the first that was ever formed in the world for that specific object." Mr. Dodge's society, the first in the world for the specific object of promoting peace, was not long allowed to remain in undisturbed possession of the field

* *Memorial of Mr. David L. Dodge*, 1854, p. 90.

† Ibid., p. 95.

‡ In 1905 Mr. Edwin D. Mead published Mr. Dodge's two tractates and prefixed an interesting biographical sketch of the author.

which it was the first to enter. Indeed, in the same year, and within the course of the next few years, peace societies in Europe as well as in the United States " were," to quote his own words, " formed, without any correspondence or knowledge of each other, the providence of God having paved the way." *

It has been thought well to state the genesis of the peace movement in the language of its founder, because Mr. Dodge can fairly be considered as such. The passages from his autobiography make it clear that what is now regarded as an economic, biological, and juridical as well as a religious movement began as a protest of highminded and deeply religious persons against war as inconsistent with the teachings of the New Testament.

In 1815, the following peace societies were created in the United States:

The New York Peace Society, the first of its kind, organized, as has been seen, by Mr. Dodge in August; the Ohio Peace Society, founded on December 2; the Massachusetts Society, founded on December 26, by the Rev. Noah Worcester, D.D., author of the tract entitled *A Solemn Review of the Custom of War* which appears to have converted Mr. Ladd to the ways of peace.

In the interval between the founding of these societies and the creation of a National Association in 1828, peace societies were formed in at least the following States: Pennsylvania, Maine, New Hampshire, Vermont, Rhode Island, Connecticut, Georgia, and North Carolina.

As Mr. Ladd said, in the interesting passage which has already been quoted, the cause of peace became the principal object of his life. He felt the necessity of gathering the various peace societies of the United States which have been mentioned into a larger and national organization to be known as the American Peace Society, which he succeeded in forming in May 1828, with the aid of the indefatigable Mr. Dodge, and of which he himself was the executive officer and for the last four years of his life its president. In the same year and month he began the *Harbinger of Peace*, which appeared monthly and had a circulation of 1,500 copies,† as the organ of the movement, and continued to edit it for three years. Its name was then changed to the *Calumet*. In 1835 it gave way to the

* Ibid., p. 99.   † Hemmenway, op. cit., p. 48.

American Advocate of Peace, which in turn became, in 1837, the *Advocate of Peace*, the monthly journal which is now, as then, the organ of the American Peace Society.

Mr. Ladd was untiring as a lecturer and writer upon his chosen subject, and in 1840 he published the *Essay on a Congress of Nations*, which is his abiding title to fame. In this remarkable essay, which will later be briefly analyzed, he advocated a Congress of Nations and a Court of Nations, each of which was to be separate and distinct, as diplomatic and judicial functions require, as he properly said, "different, not to say opposite, characters in the exercise of their functions." Thus, he said:

> I consider the Congress as the legislature, and the Court as the judiciary, in the government of nations, leaving the functions of the executive with public opinion, "the queen of the world." This division I have never seen in any essay or plan for a congress or diet of independent nations, either ancient or modern; and I believe it will obviate all the objections which have been heretofore made to such a plan.*

His many writings prove that Mr. Ladd possessed a facile pen and his style may fairly be judged by his *Essay on a Congress of Nations*. His agitation from the platform shows him to have been a ready speaker, interesting alike to the select audiences of colleges and universities, and to the simpler minded folk, who are, it is believed, a severer and a juster judge.

Hemmenway's *Memoir*, published in 1872, which is still the chief, indeed the only, account of Mr. Ladd's life, is full of tributes to his ability as a speaker and to his power to instruct, to interest, and to hold an audience. He was licensed to preach in 1837, and in a letter written some two months before his death he thus describes an experience which he and the good people of Geneva, New York, seem to have enjoyed:

> I went to Geneva, and preached three times on the Sabbath, as usual to large and attentive audiences. But my strength failed me in the last sermon, which was to an overflowing audience, and I was obliged to request the minister to give out a

---

* Advertisement, *post*, p. 1.

hymn, in the middle of the sermon which was an hour and a half long.*

The reasons for his success both in the pulpit and upon the platform are admirably stated in the following letter, written by Mr. John S. C. Abbott in 1870:

A little over forty years ago, when I was a student in the Theological Seminary at Andover, Captain Ladd addressed the young divinity students there upon the subject of peace. As I remember him, he was a florid, handsome man, looking like the bluff Christian sailor. His address was very fervent and convincing, though at this distance of time I cannot recall its details. He was received cordially by the students. His arguments were appreciated; and with no little enthusiasm, as I remember, a peace society was organized in the seminary. . . .

Upon one other occasion I met him some years after, in a social circle, in Brunswick, Maine. He was the life of the party, full of fun and frolic. I was told that his natural temperament was of the most joyous kind. He played with the children as though he were one of them. Some one pleasantly remarked, " When you become a man, you should put away childish things." He promptly replied, " Ah, I fear that I shall never be a *man*. I can never be anything more than a *Ladd*." †

The anecdote related by Mr. Abbott indicates a sense of humor which made him agreeable and persuasive in the social circle, and an interesting statement by an intimate friend shows that the humor was not confined to his friends in easy and familiar intercourse, but that it invaded, to his friend's regret, the pulpit as well. Thus the Rev. Dr. Cummings solemnly states that " If he erred at all, it was by an excess of pleasantry; or more truly perhaps, by *ill-timed* pleasantry, suffering it occasionally to break out amidst the solemn exercises of a religious meeting. This would not interfere with the edification of minds constituted like his own; but all cannot make such sudden transitions." ‡

Charles Sumner's tribute to Mr. Ladd, in his War System of the Commonwealth of Nations, is well known, and need not be quoted

---

* Hemmenway, op. cit., pp. 96-7.   † Ibid., pp. 142-3.

‡ Ibid., p. 129.

in full. In concluding his encomium, Senator Sumner felt justified
in saying:

> By a long series of practical labors, and especially by de-
> veloping, maturing, and publishing the plan of an Interna-
> tional Congress, has William Ladd enrolled himself among the
> benefactors of mankind.*

In a later portion of the address, Senator Sumner said:

> The idea of a Congress of Nations with a High Court of
> Judicature is as practicable as its consummation is confessedly
> dear to the friends of Universal Peace. Whenever this Con-
> gress is convened, as surely it will be, I know not all the names
> that will deserve commemoration in its earliest proceedings;
> but there are two, whose particular and long-continued advo-
> cacy of this Institution will connect them indissolubly with
> its fame,—the Abbé Saint-Pierre, of France, and William
> Ladd, of the United States.*

The less known but convincing tribute of the gentle and kindly
Andrew Preston Peabody, for many years Plummer Professor of
Christian Morals in Harvard University, and who knew him well
and appreciated his labors, may fittingly be quoted as placing the
man and his work in their true light. Thus, Dr. Peabody said:

> William Ladd seemed to live only for his race. He was a
> peace-maker, not merely by profession or public efforts, but in
> private life. He was not one of those who, in their love for
> the race as a whole, forget the charity due the individual. But
> he was gentle, forbearing, and conciliatory, thoughtful of the
> rights of others, always earnest to mediate between those at
> variance, ready to make sacrifice, to cherish kind feelings among
> neighbors, fellow-citizens, and fellow-Christians. Few men
> have left so many warm friends as he; and we doubt whether
> he has left an enemy; sure we are that he was no man's enemy.
> The angel of death found him as free as he was in infancy from
> malice and hatred.
> He has for years exerted a commanding influence over the
> public mind, both in our own country and abroad. When he com-

* Senator Sumner's address was delivered before the American Peace Society
May 28, 1849, and was published by the Society in 1854. The above passages
are quoted from *The Works of Charles Sumner*, 1871, vol. ii, pp. 248, 264.

menced his labors in the cause of peace, he stood almost alone.
But our friend hoped against hope, and toiled on, undaunted
by the seeming fruitlessness of his efforts. He knew that he
was laboring in the cause of God and of man, and therefore
not in vain. He has left many able and faithful fellow-workers;
but the most of them derived their first impulse from his dis-
courses or publications; and if mankind are to cease from war,
if our country is to take the lead in putting away violence
between nation and nation, his name must go down to posterity
as essentially connected with the earliest steps of this Christian
movement, and be transmitted for the lasting gratitude of his
race.*

Statesmen, clergymen, philosophers, jurists, and dreamers of
dreams, without a calling or a profession, have, from time to time,
urged upon an unwilling and unappreciative world projects of international confederation, of international conferences, and of international tribunals, and it seems desirable, before considering Mr.
Ladd's more modest proposal for a Congress of Nations, to premise
some observations upon the more meritorious or better known of
these, which have attracted attention and which have both stimu-
lated and impressed the superior minds of Europe and America.
For present purposes, it seems unnecessary to consider projects
which were drafted before the Protestant Reformation shattered
the claim of Rome even to spiritual supremacy, or before the seventeenth century which, rejecting the claims of the Empire to
universal dominion, recognized in the Congress of Westphalia
of 1648 the independence of states irrespective of origin, size
or religion, thus making possible both the society and the law of
nations.

Of seventeenth century projects, the most important are those
of Emeric Crucé (1623), of Grotius (1625), of Sully (1638), and
of William Penn (1693); and of the eighteenth century, those of
the Abbé de Saint-Pierre, of Jean Jacques Rousseau, of Jeremy
Bentham (1786-89), and of Kant (1795).

The first to be considered is " The New Cineas or Discourse of
the Occasions and Means to establish a General Peace, and the Liberty of Commerce throughout the Whole World," which was written

* Hemmenway, op. cit., pp. 130-1.

by Emeric Crucé and published in 1623.* The title suggests the existence of an old Cineas, of whom Plutarch has something to say in his *Lives of Illustrious Men*, and as the new Cineas was to show the monarchs of his day the path of wisdom just as the old Cineas had endeavored to lead Pyrrhus, famous for his dubious victories, into the ways of wisdom and peace, it seems well to consider the man Cineas and the nature of his advice, which, unfortunately, was not taken by his royal master.

Plutarch says of him:

> This person, seeing Pyrrhus eagerly preparing for Italy, led him one day when he was at leisure into the following reasonings: "The Romans, sir, are reported to be great warriors and conquerors of many warlike nations; if God permit us to overcome them, how should we use our victory?" "You ask," said Pyrrhus, "a thing evident of itself. The Romans once conquered, there is neither Greek nor barbarian city that will resist us, but we shall presently be masters of all Italy, the extent and resources and strength of which any one should rather profess to be ignorant of, than yourself." Cineas, after a little pause, "And having subdued Italy, what shall we do next?" Pyrrhus not yet discovering his intention, "Sicily", he replied, "next holds out her arms to receive us, a wealthy and populous island, and easy to be gained; for since Agathocles left it, only faction and anarchy, and the licentious violence of the demagogues prevail." "You speak," said Cineas, "what is perfectly probable, but will the possession of Sicily put an end to the war?" "God grant us," answered Pyrrhus, "victory and success in that, and we will use these as forerunners of greater things; who could forbear from Libya and Carthage then within reach, which Agathocles, even when forced to fly from Syracuse, and passing the sea only with a few ships, had all but surprised? These conquests once perfected, will any assert that of the enemies who now pretend to despise us, any one will dare to make further resistance?" "None," replied Cineas, "for then it is manifest we may with such mighty forces regain Macedon, and make an absolute conquest of Greece; and when all these are in our power, what shall

---

* Emeric Crucé, *Le Nouveau Cynée ou Discours d'Estat représentant les occasions et Moyens d'establir une Paix générale, et la liberté du commerce par tout le Monde*. In 1909 Mr. Thomas Willing Balch published a sumptuous edition of the French text and an English translation of this remarkable work. References are to the Balch ed.

we do then?" Said Pyrrhus, smiling, "We will live at our ease, my dear friend, and drink all day, and divert ourselves with pleasant conversation." When Cineas had led Pyrrhus with his argument to this point: "And what hinders us now, sir, if we have a mind to be merry, and entertain one another, since we have at hand without trouble all those necessary things, to which through much blood and great labor, and infinite hazards and mischief done to ourselves and to others, we design at last to arrive?" *

The meaning of the title of Crucé's book is thus evident, and the advice of the new fared no better than the advice of the old Cineas.

The proposal contained in this remarkable book, which had become so rare as almost to have disappeared, was that of a union of the nations and the settlement of their disputes in a general conference of their ambassadors, with the use of force if necessary to secure compliance. Although a Frenchman,† Crucé was disinterested, in the sense that he sought no special advantages for his country, his hope was to bring about and to maintain peace without aggrandizing France and his subject thus differed, as will be seen, in form as well as in substance, from the Great Design attributed to Henry IV, which, if realized, would have transferred the Austrian scepter to French hands. Crucé's desire was to secure the establishment of universal peace, and for this purpose he advocated "before resorting to arms, resort to the arbitration of the sovereign potentates and lords," ‡ apparently in an assembly composed of ambassadors, in a city chosen for this purpose—Venice was suggested—"where," to quote his language, "all sovereigns should have perpetually their ambassadors, in order that the differences that might arise should be settled by the judgment of the whole assembly. The ambassadors of those who would be interested would plead there the grievances of their masters and the other deputies would judge them without

---

* A. H. Clough's translation of *Plutarch's Lives of Illustrious Men*, 1881, vol. 2, pp. 73-4.

† Why should I a Frenchman wish harm to an Englishman, a Spaniard, or an Hindoo? I cannot wish it when I consider that they are men like me, that I am subject like them to error and sin and that all nations are bound together by a natural and, consequently, indestructible tie, which ensures that a man cannot consider another a stranger unless he follows the common and inveterate opinion that he has received from his predecessors. Crucé, loc. cit., p. 84.

‡ Ibid., p. 40.

prejudice. . . . And the better to authorize it, all the said princes will swear to hold as inviolable law what would be ordained by the majority of votes in the said assembly, and to pursue with arms those who would wish to oppose it." *

Two years after the appearance of the *Nouveau Cynée*, Grotius published the first systematic treatise on international law, entitled *De Jure Belli ac Pacis*, in which he said, influenced it may be, as Professor Nys says,† by Crucé's book:

> It would be useful, and indeed, it is almost necessary, that certain Congresses of Christian Powers should be held, in which the controversies which arise among some of them may be decided by others who are not interested; and in which measures may be taken to compel the parties to accept peace on equitable terms.‡

The plan of Grotius was not as with Crucé a union of states and a perpetual conference, but periodical conferences of independent and equal states, in which their disputes not otherwise settled were to be adjusted by diplomatic negotiations, such as happened in the Congress of Westphalia (1648), and in the Congress of Vienna (1814-15).

It is usual to begin the consideration of projects of the seventeenth century with the Great Design, composed by Sully but cunningly attributed to Henry IV; and it is eminently proper to do so, because the so-called Design of Henry IV is without question the most famous of the many projects advocating a federation of states in order to secure and to maintain peace between nations. The project is in very truth the classical project of international organization, and it has been both the inspiration and the foundation upon which

* Crucé, loc. cit., pp. 102, 122.

† In speaking of the passage of Grotius quoted above, the eminent Belgian publicist, Professor Ernest Nys, says: "We do not know what contemporary writers thought of the humanitarian theories of the *Nouveau Cynée;* it seems, however, that it exerted some influence. How are we, indeed, to explain that passage, not sufficiently illuminated, where Grotius, in his treatise upon *The Laws of War and Peace*, published two years after the *Nouveau Cynée*, extols the union and the congresses of sovereigns?" Ernest Nys, *Etudes de droit international et de droit politique*, 1896, p. 316.

‡ Grotius: *De Jure Belli ac Pacis*, Whewell's translation, vol. ii, Chap. xxiii, Sec. 8, Art. 4, p. 406.

well-wishers of their kind have, consciously or unconsciously, raised their humbler structures. The name of Henry IV is a name to conjure with, and his death at the hands of a fanatic, at the very moment when, as his friend and associate Sully asserts, he was putting himself at the head of his army to carry into effect the Great Design, has made it appear almost as the political testament of the great monarch.

A plan which Henry conceived could not be, and in fact has not been, lightly rejected, and the fact that it was, if Sully is to be trusted, upon the point of execution has impressed men so widely differing as Rousseau and Napoleon—to mention but two—with the possibility of its realization. Royalty runs better than commonfolks, a fact which Sully well knew, and in ascribing it to his royal master he prepared the minds of men for its acceptance. Still, it is not disrespectful to the memory of Henry IV to suggest that a plan fathered by a statesman such as Sully would be in itself sufficient to commend it to thoughtful consideration.

But in ascribing it to Henry IV it is fair to presume that Sully acted from no unworthy motives. Europe was in a state of expectancy at the death of Henry, and Sully sought to glorify his friend by having him fall upon the eve of the realization of great and beneficent plans, which, in Sully's opinion and in the opinion of his generation, would have immortalized the king had he been able to realize them. The important thing to be considered is not so much that the plan was not the plan of Henry, but that it ascribed to Henry views which were agitating the public mind and which had been voiced by the *New Cineas* of Crucé, which appears to have served as Sully's model.

But, before considering these two interesting and important questions, which, after all, are minor matters, it is advisable to state the purpose of the Great Design and in more detail the means by which it was to be realized. The Great Design, as sketched by Sully, contemplated the formation of a Christian republic, to be composed of fifteen states, with a general council or senate of approximately seventy persons representing the states of Europe, to deliberate on affairs as they arose, to occupy themselves with discussing different interests, to pacify quarrels, to throw light upon and oversee the civil, political, and religious affairs of Europe, whether internal

or foreign, whose decisions should have the force of irrevocable and
unchangeable decrees, as being considered to emanate from the
united authority of all the sovereigns, pronouncing as freely
as absolutely.* The object was "to divide Europe equally among
a certain number of powers, in such manner that none of them
might have cause either of envy or fear from the possessions or
power of the others," † which object, if accomplished, would result
in the interest, it was alleged, of universal peace. The political
part of the program was, to quote Sully's own words, " to divest
the House of Austria of the Empire, and of all the possessions in
Germany, Italy, and the Low Countries." ‡ That is to say, the Great
Design proposed to humble the pride and power of Austria by force,
and the federation of Europe, produced by force, was to be maintained by the sword. As Pfister has unquestionably made the most
careful examination ever made, both of the manuscripts as well as
of the printed editions of the *Economies Royales* of Sully, it seems
advisable to state in his words the brief yet adequate summary which
he has made of the Great Design:

> Henceforth, [he says] it [Europe] is divided into fifteen
> dominions, some of which are hereditary (France, Spain, Great
> Britain, Denmark, Sweden and Lombardy); others are elective,
> (the Papacy, the Empire, Poland, Hungary and Bohemia);
> lastly the republics (Venice, Switzerland, the Italian republics,
> the Republic of the Belgians). These fifteen states are reduced
> to an approximate equality of territory, of wealth, of power, and
> they form a perfect equilibrium. The same equilibrium exists
> with regard to the three religions: Catholic, Lutheran, and
> Calvinistic. Of these fifteen states, five are wholly Catholic
> (Sully does not name them), five are entirely Lutheran, and
> five Calvinistic.** These states are to form among themselves

---

* See *The Great Design of Henry IV*, ed. by Edwin D. Mead, 1909, pp. 34,
et seq.

† Ibid., p. 33.

‡ Ibid., p. 25.

** Such is, indeed, the thought of Sully, if not exactly his language. With
regard to the territories of the church, he states that neither Calvinists nor
Lutherans shall be persecuted either in person or in property, but that they shall
be "only enjoined to leave the country and to take with them their property
within a year and a day after being so ordered, or in default thereof to accept
the religion of the country." Michaud, ii, 349. Sully immediately follows
this up by adding: "A similar course shall likewise be observed with regard to

a confederation, administered by six Provincial Councils and by one General Council. The General Council is to settle disputes between the sovereign and his subjects (henceforth there will be no more revolutions!), and disputes between the states (hence no more wars in Christian Europe!). The united efforts of the confederation have but a single object; namely, to expel the Turks from Europe. The General Council is to fix the quota of troops and the taxes which each of the fifteen powers is to furnish for this new crusade. It is to levy troops and to raise money; to direct the military operations, and to apportion the conquests. When the Turk is expelled, Europe will at last enjoy this great and inestimable benefit: Universal peace.*

Pfister has shown the genesis and the growth of the Great Design by a careful and detailed study of the *Economies Royales* in comparison with the printed edition thereof, and he thus sums up his conclusions, after stating that the passages concerning the Great Design are not to be found in the original manuscript but that they were added from time to time until they assumed final form in the printed edition of 1638:

The clean-cut policy followed by Henry IV, aiming at the reduction of the House of Austria was, if I may dare to say so, the actual foundation of all these combinations. By a first exaggeration, Sully maintained that his master desired to strip Austria of its possessions in Germany, in Bohemia, and in Hungary, and to reduce Spain to the territory of the Spanish Peninsula (the version of the manuscript of the *Economies Royales*). Then he recasts the map of Europe and assigns to one or the other of the states the provinces taken from the Spanish faction. Obsessed by these hallucinations, he composes a Christian Europe of fifteen absolutely equal powers, and completely carried away by his fantasies, he finally dreams that

the kingdoms of France, of the realms of Spain, and of Great Britain, of Denmark and of Sweden, in which countries only those forms of the three religions, to the exclusion of others, may be professed which are at present permitted within them, and they shall be dealt with as hereinbefore stated." Saint-Simon had given the same interpretation of this passage, and he put the question: "How could a pope confirm the existence, the duration, and firmly establish and protect the heresies of Calvin and of Luther so that each of the heresies constitute a third of the religious unity and stand on an equality with the Catholic Religion?" *Parallèle des trois premiers rois Bourbons*, Faugère's ed., pp. 138-9.

*Charles Pfister, Les *"Economies Royales"* de Sully et le Grand Dessein de Henri IV (*Revue Historique*, 1894, vol. 56, pp. 316-7).

universal peace might reign upon this earth. The Great Project was therefore not conceived by him at one and the same time, but was formed, as it were, of successive layers reared one upon the other.*

We are now in a position to state the relation between the *New Cineas* of Crucé and the so-called *Great Design of Henry IV*, and it appears that just as the old Cineas advised Pyrrhus to rejoice his soul in peace after his conquests, so did Sully, taking a leaf from Crucé's book, essay the rôle of the new Cineas to his royal master, Henry IV. This is the conclusion reached by Pfister after a careful examination of the tractate of Crucé and of the *Great Design* of Sully. To quote Pfister's own language, "Sully shared the ideas of his time, and it was natural that after having attributed to Henry IV great designs which the latter never had, he carried the exaggeration a step further by crediting the king with the project of maintaining peace and creating a council to adjudge all differences. This last conception does not appear to us to be even original. Sully took it, it would seem, from a very curious book of the epoch, *Le Cynée d'Estat*, written by Emeric Lacroix, an author who should not be forgotten. . . . Sully did not go so far as Emeric Lacroix. He only wished peace among Christian princes, and he even excluded the Czar from his confederation because a great part of his dominions belonged to Asia and was composed of savage, barbarian, and ferocious nations. But he demanded a general council for his very Christian association as Lacroix did for the entire world. Sully did not even seek peace for the Turks. He hurled against them the united Christian world and expelled them from Europe by new crusades; and here again Sully was of his day and generation, while Lacroix looked far beyond it." †

It may seem strange, but it is nevertheless a fact that this project which contemplated an armed alliance to humble the House of Austria, to rearrange the map of Europe, and to maintain by force the status created by force, should have been considered a peace plan, and that it should be not only referred to as such, but have been taken as the model of other plans really pacific and disinterested.

* Pfister, *Les "Economies Royales,"* etc. (*Revue Historique*, 1894, vol. 56, p. 318). † Ibid., pp. 330-1.

The influence of the *Great Design* upon subsequent thought has been such as to justify this somewhat detailed account of its origin and of its authorship. William Penn refers to it as justifying his scheme, saying:

> I will not then fear to be censured for proposing an expedient for the present and future peace of Europe, when it was not only the design but glory of one of the greatest princes that ever reigned in it.

The Abbé de Saint-Pierre specifically calls his project " The Abridgment of the Project of Universal Peace invented by King Henry the Great."

After showing the influence of the Great Design, Pfister says that the ideas of the Abbé de Saint-Pierre, which were admittedly based upon the Great Design, were in 1795 " taken up again, arranged and formulated by the greatest of modern philosophers," adding " Is it not curious that, indirectly, the *Economies Royales* of Sully exercised an important influence upon the ethical system of Immanuel Kant." * It is indeed curious, but greatest and strangest of all is the influence which the Great Design apparently exercised upon the great Napoleon. Thus Count de Las Cases, in his " Memorial of St. Helena," quotes the Emperor as saying:

> One of my greatest ideas was the bringing together and the concentration of the peoples forming a geographical unit which revolution and policy had broken up and cut to pieces. Thus, though scattered, there are in Europe more than 30,000,000 Frenchmen, 15,000,000 Spaniards, 15,000,000 Italians, 30,000,000 Germans, and of each of these peoples I would fain have made a separate and distinct nation. . . .
>
> After this summary simplification, it would have been easier to give one's self up to the beautiful dream of civilization; for in such a state of things there would have been a greater chance of bringing about everywhere a unity of codes, of principles, of opinions, of sentiments, of views, and of interests. Then, perhaps, under the ægis of universal enlightenment, it would have been possible to conceive of an Amphictyonic assembly of Greece, or of an American Congress for the European family of nations.†

* Ibid., p. 334.

† Las Cases' *Mémorial de Sainte-Hélène*, 1823, vol. 4, pt. 7, pp. 125-6.

Upon this passage, summarized, but not quoted, in his masterly *Confederation of Europe,* Mr. Phillips says: "Whether this plan had ever been seriously contemplated or not, it is easy to recognize in it the source of its inspiration." *

In 1693 the gentle Penn published an *Essay towards the Present and Future Peace of Europe,* proposing the establishment of a European diet, parliament, or estates, moved thereto, as he says, by the project of Henry IV. The sovereign princes of Europe were to be represented in the diet, according to their revenues, not upon the plane of equality. The diet itself was to meet yearly, or every second or third year. The diet, or assembly, was to be called the sovereign, or imperial, diet, parliament, or estate of Europe, "before which sovereign assembly, should be brought all differences depending between one sovereign and another, that cannot be made up by private embassies, before the sessions begin." †

It occurred to the generous author that the sovereign Princes might prefer to settle their disputes by arms instead of submitting them to the diet, or that, if submitted, they might fail to execute the judgments of the assembly. To meet these various contingencies, he therefore provided that, " if any of the Sovereignties that constitute these imperial States, shall refuse to submit their claim or pretensions to them, or to abide and perform the judgment thereof, and seek their remedy by arms, or delay their compliance beyond the time prefixed in their resolutions, all the other Sovereignties, united as one strength, shall compel the submission and performance of the sentence, with damages to the suffering party, and charges to the Sovereignties that obligated their submission." †

It would seem that the Congress of Nations contemplated by Penn was to settle by diplomats, not necessarily by judges trained in the law, disputes of all kinds whatsoever, whether they were justiciable or non-justiciable. A distinction does not seem to be drawn between these two categories, so that diplomats would or might pass upon and determine each. But however highly we may appreciate the diplomat

---

* Walter Alison Phillips' *The Confederation of Europe: A Study of the European Alliance, 1813-1823, as an Experiment in the International Organization of Peace,* 1914, p. 20.

† William Penn, *An Essay towards the Present and Future Peace of Europe,* sec. iv.

in his proper sphere, the wisdom of mankind has established courts of justice for the settlement of justiciable questions. A further objection to Penn's project is the unequal representation of the states, for equality before the law is as true of nations as of individuals. Finally, the project seems to contain within it the germs of a league to enforce peace and of an international police which would make it objectionable to those who believe in public opinion as a sanction of law, whereas the provision for the use of force will commend it to those who believe in force as the sanction of law.

The chief projects of the eighteenth century are, as has been said, those of the Abbé de Saint-Pierre, Jean Jacques Rousseau, Jeremy Bentham, and Immanuel Kant.

The purpose of the Abbé de Saint-Pierre is indicated in the title, Perpetual Peace, which he gave to the various editions of his project. In the year 1712 he published anonymously, at Cologne, a volume small enough to be slipped in the pocket, but weighty in thought and purpose, entitled " Memoirs to Render Peace Perpetual in Europe." This is in the nature of an essay or of a first sketch. In the two-volume edition of his treatise, published in 1713, he states the relation of his project to that of Henry IV, and in the third volume, which appeared in 1717, this relation appears in the title. He informs us in the preface to the first volume of the enlarged edition that a friend, to whom he had shown the first sketch, informed him that " Henry IV had formed a project similar in substance. In the Memoirs of the Duke of Sully, his Prime Minister, and in the history of his reign by Mr. de Perefixe, I even found that this project had already been agreed to and approved by a large number of sovereigns at the commencement of the past century." *

The title to the third volume, which appeared in 1717, not only points out the relationship, but mentions the success with which, as Sully would have us believe, the Great Design of Henry IV had been crowned. The first sentence of the title thus defines the good Abbé's purpose: " Project of a treaty to render peace perpetual between Christian sovereigns and to maintain constantly free commerce between the nations to strengthen in greater degree the sovereign houses upon the throne." The second part of the title is evidently

---

* Abbé de Saint-Pierre's *Projet pour rendre la Paix perpétuelle en Europe* (1713), vol. 1, p. ix.

to convince the reader by the mere title page of the feasibility of the scheme, as he declares it to have been " proposed formally by Henry, the great king of France, agreed to by Queen Elizabeth, by James I, King of England, her successor, and by most of the other potentates of Europe."

Just as Sully had obtained a hearing for the Great Design, by ascribing it to Henry IV, so Saint-Pierre obtained a hearing for his Project of Perpetual Peace by declaring it to be substantially the Great Design of Henry IV. In 1728 Saint-Pierre published an abridgment of the project, which the title declares to have been " invented by King Henry the Great, approved by Queen Elizabeth, by King James, her successor, by the republics, and divers other potentates, adapted to the present state of affairs in Europe."

Without attempting in this place a comparison between the Great Design and Saint-Pierre's Perpetual Peace, the purpose of the first was to create by force of arms a new state of affairs in Europe, and to maintain, by force if necessary, the equilibrium thus brought about by force. The Abbé de Saint-Pierre believed that it was not necessary to make Europe over by force, but to procure, by force if necessary, the acceptance of the status created by the Treaty of Westphalia of 1648 and of Utrecht of 1713-14, in the conclusion of which he was interested as secretary to the French plenipotentiary. In simplest terms, the Abbé's project was to maintain the *status quo*, which could, in his opinion, be done by a treaty of alliance, consisting of twelve fundamental provisions which he stated in the form of a treaty, and which in his opinion only needed signature in order to be effective. Peace was thus to be ushered in by a stroke of the pen.

The project of the Abbé de Saint-Pierre was, as has been stated, based upon the Great Design of Henry IV and contemplated a union, if possible, of all Christian sovereigns, with a perpetual congress or senate in which the sovereigns should be represented by deputies. The union was, in the first instance, to be voluntary, but after enough states had joined it to make fourteen votes, a sovereign refusing to enter was to be declared an enemy to the repose of Europe, and force was to be used against him until he adhered to it or until he was entirely despoiled of his territories. The organ of the union, called the Senate, was to consist of some four and twenty members, and before this body complaints of the sovereign members of the union were to be laid. The dispute was to be decided by the senate provisionally by a majority, finally by three-fourths of the members, and the failure of a sovereign or members of the union to accept the decision required the European society or union to declare war against the recalcitrant member and to continue it until he was disarmed, the judgment executed, the costs of the war paid by him, and the country conquered from him forever separated from his dominions. The purpose which Saint-Pierre had in mind was thus to confederate Europe by means of a treaty to be signed by the representatives of European powers, and the project itself has the form of a treaty for such signature. He regarded the treaty of Utrecht, which framed and contained the provisions of the treaty of Westphalia, as creating a satisfactory state of affairs, and his confederation was intended to perpetuate the status created by these treaties; and by the creation of a senate to legislate for members of the union and to decide conflicts arising among them he hoped to prevent a resort to arms, as by express agreement wars between the members of the union were to be renounced.

Such is, in summary terms, Saint-Pierre's project for perpetual peace, and it is perhaps possible to estimate the value of the plan by this simple statement of its provisions, but in view of the very great influence exercised by the Abbé's project—for, as pointed out by our countryman, Henry Wheaton, in his *History of the Law of Nations*,* and by the distinguished German publicist, von Holtzendorff, in his " Idea of Perpetual World Peace ", † its main provisions were incorporated in the German confederation of 1815, and as pointed out by Mr. Phillips in his " Confederation of Europe ",‡

* In speaking of the abridged plan of Saint-Pierre, published in 1729, reduced to five fundamental articles, Wheaton says that " the almost verbal coincidence of these articles with those of the fundamental act of the Germanic confederation established by the Congress of Vienna in 1815 is remarkable." Wheaton's *History of the Law of Nations in Europe and America*, 1845, p. 263.

† " The project of the Abbé de Saint-Pierre is of great interest from various standpoints. One would be inclined to maintain that its author had a presentiment of the Germanic confederation of 1815." Franz v. Holtzendorff's *Die Idee des ewigen Völkerfriedens* (*Sammlung gemeinverständlicher wissenschaftlicher Vorträge*, 1882, vol. xvii, p. 687).

‡ Speaking of the Great Design, Mr. Phillips says, " It inspired the *Projet de Paix perpétuelle* of the Abbé de Saint-Pierre, and through him the Emperor

the Abbé's project was, it would seem, the inspiration of the Holy Alliance—it is advisable to state the fundamental articles of Saint-Pierre's plan, twelve in number, which could only be changed by unanimous consent, omitting the " important articles ", eight in number, and the " useful articles ", likewise eight in number, which could be changed at any time by a three-fourths vote of the senate.

The fundamental articles are:

1. The present Sovereigns, by their undersigned Deputies, have agreed to the following Articles. There shall be from this day forward a Society, a permanent and perpetual Union between the undersigned Sovereigns, and, if possible, among all Christian Sovereigns, to preserve unbroken peace in Europe. . . .

The Sovereigns shall be perpetually represented by their Deputies in a perpetual Congress or Senate in a free city.

2. The European Society shall not at all interfere with the Government of any State, except to preserve its constitution, and to render prompt and adequate assistance to rulers and chief magistrates against seditious persons and rebels. . . .

3. The Union shall employ its whole strength and care in order, during regencies, minorities, or feeble reigns, to prevent injury to the Sovereign, either in his person or prerogatives, or to the Sovereign House, and in case of such shall send Commissioners to inquire into the facts, and troops to punish the guilty. . . .

4. Each Sovereign shall be contented, he and his successors, with the Territory he actually possesses, or which he is to possess by the accompanying Treaty. . . . No Sovereign, nor member of a Sovereign Family, can be Sovereign of any State besides that or those which are actually in the possession of his family. The annuities which the Sovereigns owe to the private persons of another State shall be paid as heretofore. No Sovereign shall assume the title of Lord of any Country of which he is not in possession, and the Sovereigns shall not make an exchange of Territory or sign any Treaty among themselves except by a majority of the four-and-twenty votes of the Union, which shall remain guarantee for the execution of reciprocal promises.

Alexander I.'s idea of a universal Holy Alliance. . . . It is impossible to examine this project without being struck by the fact that there is scarcely one of its provisions which does not emerge, at least as a subject of debate among the Powers, during the years of European reconstruction after 1814 " (Phillips, op. cit., pp. 19, 22-23).

5. No Sovereign shall henceforth possess two Sovereignties, either hereditary or elective, except that the Electors of the Empire may be elected Emperors, so long as there shall be Emperors. If by right of succession there should fall to a Sovereign a State more considerable than that which he possesses, he may leave that which he possesses, and settle himself on that which is fallen to him.

6. The Kingdom of Spain shall not go out of the House of Bourbon, . . .

7. The Deputies shall incessantly labor to codify all the Articles of Commerce in general, and between different nations in particular; but in such a manner that the laws may be equal and reciprocal towards all nations, and founded upon Equity. The Articles which shall have been passed by a majority of the votes of the original deputies, shall be executed provisionally according to their Form and Tenor, till they be amended and improved by three-fourths of the votes, when a greater number of members shall have signed the Union.

The Union shall establish in different towns Chambers of Commerce, consisting of Deputies authorized to reconcile, and to judge strictly and without Appeal, the disputes that shall arise either in relation to Commerce or others matters, between the subjects of different Sovereigns, in value above ten thousand pounds; the other suits, of less consequence, shall be decided, as usual, by the judges of the place where the defendant lives. Each Sovereign shall lend his hand to the execution of the judgments of the Chambers of Commerce, as if they were his own judgments.

Each Sovereign shall, at his own charge, exterminate his inland robbers and banditti, and the pirates on his coasts, upon pain of making reparation; and if he has need of help, the Union shall assist him.

8. No Sovereign shall take up arms, or commit any hostility, but against him who shall be declared an enemy to the European Society. But if he has any cause to complain of any of the Members, or any demand to make upon them, he shall order his Deputy to present a memorial to the Senate in the City of Peace, and the Senate shall take care to reconcile the difference by its mediating Commissioners; or, if they cannot be reconciled, the Senate shall judge them by arbitral judgment, by majority of votes provisionally, and by three-fourths of the votes definitely. This judgment shall not be given until each Senator shall have received the instructions and orders of his master upon that point, and until he shall have communicated them to the Senate.

The Sovereign who shall take up arms before the Union has declared war, or who shall refuse to execute a regulation of the Society, or a judgment of the Senate, shall be declared an enemy to the Society, and it shall make war upon him, until he be disarmed, and until its judgment and regulations be executed, and he shall even pay the charges of the war, and the country that shall be conquered from him at the close of hostilities shall be forever separated from his dominions.

If, after the Society is formed to the number of fourteen votes, a Sovereign should refuse to enter thereinto, it shall declare him an enemy to the repose of Europe, and shall make war upon him until he enter into it, or until he be entirely despoiled.

9. There shall be in the Senate of *Europe* four-and-twenty Senators or Deputies of the United Sovereigns, neither more nor less, namely:—*France, Spain, England, Holland, Savoy, Portugal, Bavaria* and Associates, *Venice, Genoa* and Associates, *Florence* and Associates, *Switzerland* and Associates, *Lorrain* and Associates, *Sweden, Denmark, Poland*, the Pope, *Muscovy, Austria, Courland* and Associates, *Prussia, Saxony, Palatine* and Associates, *Hanover* and Associates, Ecclesiastical Electors and Associates. Each Deputy shall have but one vote.

10. The Members and Associates of the Union shall contribute to the expenses of the Society, and to the subsidies for its security, each in proportion to his revenues, and to the riches of his people, and everyone's quota shall at first be regulated provisionally by a majority, and afterwards by three-fourths of the votes, when the Commissioners of the Union shall have taken, in each State, what instructions and information shall be necessary thereupon; and if anyone is found to have paid too much provisionally, it shall afterwards be made up to him, both in principal and interest, by those who shall have paid too little. The less powerful Sovereigns and Associates in forming one vote, shall alternately nominate their Deputy in proportion to their quotas.

11. When the Senate shall deliberate upon anything pressing and imperative for the security of the Society, either to prevent or quell sedition, the question may be decided by a majority of votes provisionally, and, before it is deliberated upon, they shall begin by deciding, by majority, whether the matter is imperative.

12. None of the eleven fundamental Articles above named shall be in any point altered, without the *unanimous* consent of all the members; but as for the other Articles, the Society may

always, by three-fourths of the votes, add or diminish, for the common good, whatever it shall think fit.*

In the preface to the Project the Abbé de Saint-Pierre makes several very wise remarks, which have not yet lost their aptness. Thus he says, " The present constitution of Europe can only produce almost continuous wars, because it can never have sufficient guaranty of the execution of treaties." And again, he calls attention to the impossibility of peace based upon the principle of equilibrium, thus: " The balance of power between the House of France and the House of Austria cannot result in a sufficient guaranty against foreign wars nor against civil wars, and consequently cannot result in sufficient security either for the preservation of nations or the preservation of commerce." †

It has been said that the Abbé's plan forecast the Germanic confederation of 1815, and not unnaturally so, because the project itself was based upon the Abbé's conception of the Germanic corps, as he calls it, and indeed he draws the comparison, on the one hand, between the Germanic corps, which existed in his time, and the European corps, which he hoped to call into being. Continuing, the Abbé de Saint-Pierre says that " the same motives and the same means which have sufficed formerly for a permanent society of all the sovereignties of Germany are within the reach and at the disposal of the sovereigns of to-day, and may suffice for the formation of a permanent society of all the Christian sovereignties of Europe." ‡ The possibility of this he bases upon the fact that " the approbation which most of the sovereigns of Europe gave to the project of the European society proposed to them by Henry IV [called by Saint-Pierre, Henry the Great] justifies us in hoping that a like project will be approved by their successors." ‡

After making the above statements, the good Abbé puts his entire case in the form of a premise: " If the European Society herein proposed can procure to the Christian princes sufficient surety of a perpetual peace within and beyond their estates, there is none

---

* The above translation is taken from W. Evans Darby, *International Tribunals*, 4th ed., 1904, pp. 70-6. The original French text is to be found in *Projet pour rendre la Paix perpétuelle en Europe*, 1713, vol. 1, pp. 284-356.

† Ibid., p. vi.

‡ Ibid., p. x.

of them to whom it would not be a greater advantage to sign a treaty for the establishment of this society than not to sign it." He next states as a fact that, " The European society herein proposed can procure to the crown princes sufficient guaranty of a perpetual peace within and without their estates." This being the case, he draws the logical conclusion that " there will be none of them to whom it will not be more advantageous to sign the treaty for the establishment of the society than not to sign it." *

Abbé Saint-Pierre's project has been stated at very considerable length, and the twelve fundamental articles quoted in his own words. His reasons for believing that his project would be successful have likewise been stated in his own language, for the twofold reason that the project was a serious, high-minded and wholly disinterested attempt to establish a permanent peace by means of a European society or union based upon the maintenance of the then existing status. Therein lay its strength and its weakness—its strength, because the sovereigns of Europe would be more inclined to sign a treaty guaranteeing them their thrones, their possessions and the rights of their successors against war from without and rebellion from within; its weakness, because it precluded the possibility of change, and change is apparently the one constant factor in the world's history. It closed the door to the ambition of the sovereign who might wish to increase his dominions, and it blighted the hope of the people who might wish to change their sovereigns or their forms of government, and by so doing better their own condition.

Rousseau was indeed a friendly critic of the project, but he criticized the Abbé for having appealed to the intelligence and judgment of the princes of Europe, instead of making the lower appeal to their interests, in a passage which well deserves quotation:

> I would not dare [he said] to reply with the Abbé de Saint-Pierre that the veritable glory of princes consists in advancing the interests and the happiness of their subjects; that all their interests are subordinated to their reputation, and that the reputation which is acquired with the wise depends upon the good which we do to our fellow beings; that perpetual peace being the greatest of all undertakings, and the most likely to cover its author with immortal glory, this undertaking, being the

* Projet pour rendre la Paix perpétuelle en Europe, vol. 1, pp. xiii-xiv.

most useful, is therefore the most honorable to sovereigns, the only one which is not stained with blood, rapine, tears, and maledictions; and finally, the surest way of obtaining distinction among the mob of kings is to work for the public good. Let us leave to the demagogues such reasons, which in the cabinets of the ministers overwhelmed with ridicule the author of these projects, but let us not despise, like them, his arguments, and whatever may be the virtue of princes, let us rather discourse of their interests.*

The great philosopher Leibnitz, to whom the Abbé de Saint-Pierre had sent his project, wrote in reply, " I have read carefully the Project of Permanent Peace for Europe, which the Abbé de St. Pierre has done me the honor to send me, and I am persuaded that such a proposal, taken as a whole, is feasible, and that its execution would be one of the most useful things in the world. Although my support is not worth much, I have thought that my sense of obligation compels me not to withhold it, but to add some remarks of my own for the satisfaction of an author of such merit, who must have had much force of character and firmness to have dared, and been able, to oppose with success the crowd of prejudices and the taunts of mockery." †

Leibnitz, however, considered that the subordination of the empire was a serious defect, and he proceeded to point out two respects in which the system of the empire was superior to that suggested by Saint-Pierre. In the first place, Leibnitz stated that the tribunal of the imperial chamber (Reichskammergericht) consists of judges and assessors free to follow their consciences without being bound by the instructions of the princes and states nominating them, and in the second place, he objected that, in the Abbé's project there was no provision for hearing the complaints of subjects against their sovereigns, whereas in the empire subjects could plead against their princes or their magistrates.

" The comment of Leibnitz is interesting ", says Mr. Phillips, " because it anticipates the objection which, a hundred years later, Castlereagh considered fatal to the system of guarantees, precisely similar to that suggested in the third article of St. Pierre's project, which

* *Extrait du projet de paix perpétuelle de M. l'Abbé de Saint-Pierre, Oeuvres complètes de J. J. Rousseau*, P. Pourrat Frères, Paris, 1832, vol. 6, pp. 432-3.
† Darby, op. cit., p. 98.

the reactionary powers sought to formulate at Aix-la-Chapelle and did formulate in the Troppau Protocol. The Abbé de Saint-Pierre pointed out how the proposals in this article would not weaken but strengthen the princes, by guaranteeing to each of them 'not only their states against all foreign invasion, but also their authority against all rebellions of their subjects.' In a Memorandum on the treaties presented to the powers at Aix-la-Chapelle, Castlereagh wrote:

> The idea of an *Alliance Solidaire* by which each state shall be bound to support the state of succession, government and possession within all other states from violence and attack, upon condition of receiving for itself a similar guarantee, must be understood as morally implying the previous establishment of such a system of general government as may secure and enforce upon all kings and nations an internal system of peace and justice. Till the mode of constructing such a system shall be devised, the consequence is inadmissible, as nothing could be more immoral, or more prejudicial to the character of government generally, than the idea that their force was collectively to be prostituted to the support of established power, without any consideration of the extent to which it was abused.

"In writing this," Mr. Phillips continues, "Castlereagh was unconsciously repeating and expanding a comment on the Abbé's third article made long before by Rousseau, who in his *Jugement sur la paix perpétuelle* had written: 'One cannot guarantee princes against the revolt of their subjects without at the same time guaranteeing subjects against the tyranny of princes. Otherwise the institution could not possibly survive.' " *

Partisans of peace projects insist that their plans are feasible and that their critics are not justified in denouncing them as impracticable, because until they have been tried it cannot be known that they would fail. This plea for the suspension of judgment cannot be granted the Saint-Pierre, because, as Wheaton and Holtzendorff have stated, the project was tried in the Germanic Confederation of 1815 and it failed, and as Mr. Phillips has pointed out in his *Confederation of Europe*, Abbé Saint-Pierre's principles were weighed and found wanting in the Holy Alliance. Saint-Pierre's project is never-

* Phillips, op. cit., pp. 24-5.

theless interesting and important, because, as Holtzendorff has said, and truly, " His plan limits in reality and with tolerable accuracy the field within which, at least since the end of the former century, the discussion concerning the possibility of perpetual peace has in its essentials taken place." *

It is usual to consider Rousseau's project of perpetual peace, but it will not be necessary in this connection to dwell upon it at length, because it is in reality an analysis and justification of Saint-Pierre's views, uncouthly expressed by the author but exquisitely expressed by Rousseau.

Rousseau lays down three premises from which he draws the conclusion that peace is possible. These premises are (1) that with the exception of Turkey there prevails among all the peoples of Europe a social connection, imperfect but more compact than the general and loose ties of humanity; (2) that the imperfection of this society makes the condition of those who compose it worse than would be the deprivation of all society amongst them; (3) that those primary bonds which render this society harmful make it at the same time easily capable of improvement, so that all its members may derive their happiness from that which actually constitutes their misery, and change the state of war which prevails among them into an abiding peace.

How can this be done? Rousseau disregards the twelve fundamental articles of the Abbé's project and thus restates the five articles which replaced them in Saint-Pierre's abridgment of the original project: That the contracting sovereigns shall establish a perpetual and irrevocable alliance, and shall name their plenipotentiaries in a diet or permanent congress in which all the differences of the contracting parties shall be adjusted by arbitration or by judicial decisions (Article 1); that the number of sovereigns shall be specified whose plenipotentiaries shall have the right to vote in the diet, those who shall be invited to accede to the treaty, the order, the time and the manner by which the presidency shall pass from one to another for an equal period, and finally the quota of contributions of money and the manner of assessing them to meet the common expenses (Article 2); that the confederation shall guarantee to each of its members the possession and government of their territories according to actual

---

* *Die Idee des ewigen Völkerfriedens,* loc. cit., pp. 19-20.

possession and the treaties then in effect, that disputes arising between them should be settled by the diet, and that the members of the diet should renounce the right to settle their disputes by force and also renounce the right to make war on one another (Article 3); that the member violating the fundamental treaty should be placed under the ban of Europe and prescribed as a common enemy, that is to say, if it refuses to execute the judgments of the diet, if it makes preparations for war, if it takes up arms to resist or to attack any of the allies, it should be proceeded against by the allies and reduced to obedience (Article 4); that the provisional decisions of the diet should be by a majority, the final decisions requiring a majority of three-fourths of the members of the diet acting under instructions from their governments, that the diet could legislate for the well-being of Europe, but could not change any of the provisions of the fundamental articles without the unanimous consent of the contracting powers (Article 5).*

In essence Rousseau's plan is that of Saint-Pierre, and indeed Rousseau specifically disclaimed originality. He had undertaken to arrange and to edit the papers and printed works of the good Abbé, and the project which bears his name is in reality the Abbé's with such comments as occurred to him in his analysis and exposition of the Abbé's project.

Nothing is more common in books of political theory than the statement that Rousseau was incompetent in matters political, and yet his *Social Contract* has profoundly influenced government as well as authorities of government, and its main propositions cannot be gainsaid, especially in the Americas, where the peoples have separated themselves from Europe and created states to their liking, and where they have changed governments and forms of government whenever they have felt disposed to do so.†

Rousseau abridged or restated the Abbé de Saint-Pierre's project

---

* *Extrait du projet de Paix perpétuelle de M. l'Abbé de Saint-Pierre*, loc. cit., pp. 423-5.

† Wheaton was a man of affairs as well as a theorist, and he says in his *History of the Law of Nations in Europe and America* that "Rousseau published in 1761 a little work to which he modestly gave the title of *Extrait du Projet de Paix perpétuelle de M. l'Abbé de Saint-Pierre*, but which is stamped with the marks of Rousseau's peculiar original genius as a system-builder and reasoner upon the problem of social science." (P. 264.)

of a perpetual peace, prefixing to it a masterly introduction, and he
followed it up with a criticism called the " Judgment on the Perpetual
Peace," in which he laid his finger not merely upon the weakness of
Saint-Pierre's project but upon the simplicity of the good Abbé in
imagining that princes could be counted upon to do the right thing
if it were only shown them. Rousseau was hardly less a dreamer
than Saint-Pierre but he realized that, if dreams were to be put into
effect by princes and the great of the world, it could only be done
by appealing to the motives that influence them, namely, their ambition and their self-interest.

In his " Judgment on the Perpetual Peace ", Rousseau says:

> In regard to the disputes between prince and prince, can we
> hope to subject men to a superior tribunal who dare boast that
> they only hold their powers by the sword, and who only mention
> God himself because he is in heaven? Will sovereigns submit
> their quarrels to judicial solution when the rigor of the laws has
> never been able to force private citizens to do so in their own
> cases? A simple gentleman who has sustained an injury dis-
> dains to carry his complaints before the court of the marshals
> of France, and do you wish that a king should lay his before a
> European diet? There is, moreover, this difference, that one
> sins against the laws and doubly exposes his life, whereas the
> other only exposes his subjects; that he employs, in taking up
> arms, a right admitted by every human being, and for which
> he claims to be responsible to God alone. . . .
> Incessantly misled by the appearance of things, princes will
> reject, then, this peace when they weigh their interests them-
> selves; what will be the result when these interests are weighed
> by their ministers, whose needs are always opposed to those
> of the people and almost always to those of the prince? Minis-
> ters need war to make them indispensable, to embarrass the
> prince so that he cannot extricate himself without their aid,
> and to ruin the state if necessary rather than that they should
> lose their places. . . .
> Nor must we believe with the Abbé de Saint-Pierre that even
> with good-will, which neither princes nor their ministers will
> ever have, it would be easy to find a favorable moment for the
> execution of this system, as it would be necessary in such a
> case that the sum of private interests should not outweigh the
> common interest, and that each should believe he saw in the
> well-being of all the greatest good to be hoped for himself.
> Now, this demands a union of wisdom in so many heads and a

union of relations in so many interests that we can hardly hope for a fortuitous union of all the necessary circumstances. However, if this agreement does not happen there is only force to take its place, in which event it is no longer a question of persuading but of compelling, and instead of writing books we must raise troops.

Thus, although the project might be very wise, the means of executing it betrayed the simplicity of the author. He imagined in his goodness that it was only necessary to assemble a congress and propose therein his articles, that they would be signed and that all would be ended. Let us admit that in all the projects of this honest man he saw well enough the effect of things when they were established, but that his judgment was that of a child as to the means of putting them into effect.

I do not need to add more to prove that the project of the Christian republic is not chimerical than to name its first author, for assuredly Henry IV was neither a fool nor Sully a visionary.*

The value of Rousseau's plan consists in the skill with which he justified the Abbé's purpose, and if the arguments which he himself advances do not warrant the confederation, they do at least justify the international organization of a looser kind for the negotiation of treaties and the settlement of disputes peaceably by proper agencies.

Bentham's " Plan for an Universal and Perpetual Peace " appears to have been written between 1786 and 1789, but it was first published in 1839. In justification of it he says, " The happiest of mankind are sufferers by war; and the wisest, nay, even the least wise, are wise enough to ascribe the chief of their sufferings to that cause." The project consists of some fourteen articles, to which are prefixed " two fundamental propositions:—1. The reduction and fixation of the force of the several nations that compose the European system; 2. The emancipation of the distant dependencies of each state." † In the matter of armament it may be said that the distinguished reformer was of the opinion that " general and perpetual treaties might be formed, limiting the number of troops to be maintained." The chief proposal to maintain the peace after the limitation of armament and the emancipation of distant depen-

* Rousseau's *Jugement sur la Paix perpétuelle*, loc. cit., vol. 6, pp. 452-6.

† *Principles of International Law*, essay iv, Bowring's ed. of *The Works of Jeremy Bentham*, pt. viii, p. 546.

dencies was " by the establishment of a common court of judicature for the decision of differences between the several nations, although such a court were not to be armed with any coercive powers." * The creation and operation of such a court was, in his opinion, the necessary complement of the reduction of armament, because war is the consequence of difference of opinion between two nations, because there is no tribunal common to them. " Establish a common tribunal," he says, " the necessity for war no longer follows from difference of opinion. Just or unjust, the decision of the arbiters will save the credit, the honor of the contending party." † The tribunal contemplated by Bentham was apparently a diplomatic body, which he calls a congress or diet, and which he says " might be constituted by each power sending two deputies to the place of meeting: one of these to be the principal, the other to act as an occasional substitute." The proceedings of the congress or diet were to be public, and " its power would consist ", to quote his own language, " 1. In reporting its opinion; 2. In causing that opinion to be circulated in the dominions of each state; . . . 3. After a certain time, in putting the refractory state under the ban of Europe." It will be seen that Bentham contemplated the use of force, for in commenting upon the third point he says, " There might, perhaps, be no harm in regulating, as a last resource, the contingent to be furnished by the several states for enforcing the decrees of the court." He felt, however, that a free press could be trusted to create a public opinion in behalf of compliance with the judgments of the court, and that the resort to force would be unnecessary.

It would seem that Bentham had in mind the submission to the congress or diet of all disputes between nations, although it might be inferred that in the use of the term judicature or court Bentham was speaking of justiciable disputes. However that may be, the plan in its entirety was nullified by the prerequisites, for nations are unwilling to renounce colonies, even though they may be the source of war, and disarmament or the limitation thereof will no doubt continue to be unacceptable until a satisfactory substitute has been proposed for war and incorporated in the practice of nations.

The philosopher Kant was no doubt influenced by the Treaty of Rastatt, which had just been negotiated at the Congress of Bâle

* Ibid., p. 547.   † Ibid., p. 552.

in 1795, just as the Abbé de Saint-Pierre's project was due to the Congress of Utrecht of 1714-15. Both are in the form of treaties. The philosopher of Königsberg drafted six preliminary articles, the acceptance of which he believed to be essential to perpetual peace. They were interesting in his day and generation, and they are as timely to-day as when first drafted, although they are likely to wait many a day for their acceptance. They are therefore quoted in full, without comment, as comment seems unnecessary:

1. No treaty of peace shall be regarded as valid, if made with the secret reservation of material for a future war.

2. No state having an independent existence—whether it be great or small—shall be acquired by another through inheritance, exchange, purchase or donation.

3. Standing armies (*miles perpetuus*) shall be abolished in course of time.

4. No national debts shall be contracted in connection with the external affairs of the state.

5. No state shall violently interfere with the constitution and administration of another.

6. No state at war with another shall countenance such modes of hostility as would make mutual confidence impossible in a subsequent state of peace: such are the employment of assassins (*percussores*) or of poisoners (*venefici*), breaches of capitulation, the instigating and making use of treachery (*perduellio*) in the hostile state.*

Kant considered that to secure perpetual peace the civil constitution of every state must be republican and that all international right must be grounded upon a federation of free states. The term " republican " as used by Kant is, however, to be understood as synonymous with representative government, and he believed that neither a despotism nor a democracy would prevent war, but that representatives of the people could be trusted to pass upon the question of war and peace reasonably. We have unfortunately learned that constitutional, in the sense of representative, government does not necessarily have the effect which Kant hoped it would have. A confederation of states was, in the philosopher's opinion, requisite to international peace. It should be observed, however, that it is a federation of free states;

* *Perpetual Peace, A Philosophical Essay by Immanuel Kant, 1795*, translation of M. Campbell Smith, 1915, pp. 107-14.

that is to say, a federation in which the states do not lose their identity or their sovereign prerogatives, and Kant was very careful to point out that it was not to be a permanent confederation. It was to be brought about by the free consent of the states desiring to enter into it, and continuance in it was likewise to be voluntary. Kant's language on this point is so important as to suggest quotation, and in view of the peace conferences which have been called by the Czar of Russia and which have met at The Hague, although unfortunately not at stated periods, Kant's reference to The Hague has much more than a passing interest. However, he should be allowed to speak for himself, which he does as follows:

> Such a general association of states, having for its object the preservation of peace, might be termed the permanent congress of nations. Such was the diplomatic conference formed at The Hague during the first part of the eighteenth century, with a similar view, consisting of the ministers of the greater part of the European courts and even of the smallest republics. In this manner all Europe was constituted into one federal state, of which the several members submitted their differences to the decision of this conference as their sovereign arbiter. . . .
>
> What we mean to propose is a general congress of nations, of which both the meeting and the duration are to depend entirely on the sovereign wills of the several members of the league, and not an indissoluble union like that which exists between the several states of North America founded on a municipal constitution. Such a congress and such a league are the only means of realizing the idea of a true public law, according to which the differences between nations would be determined by civil proceedings as those between individuals are determined by civil judicature, instead of resorting to war, a mean of redress worthy only of barbarians.*

Kant does not work out in detail the idea of a congress, meeting from time to time, to agree upon principles of international law, nor does he suggest the establishment of an international court to administer the law which the practice and the custom of nations has made, or which has been agreed to in the Congress of Nations. Both these ideas present themselves to the mind of the reader, even

---

* *Rechtslehre*, pt. 2, sec. 61 (*Immanuel Kant's Sämmtliche Werke*, Rosenkranz and Schubert ed., 1838, pt. 9, p. 204) ; Wheaton, op. cit., p. 754.

though they may not have been formulated and expressed by Kant, who only says that

> If it be a duty to cherish the hope that the universal dominion of public law may ultimately be realized, by a gradual but continued progress, the establishment of perpetual peace to take the place of those mere suspensions of hostility called treaties of peace, is not a mere chimera, but a problem, of which time, abridged by the uniform and continual progress of the human mind, will ultimately furnish a satisfactory solution.*

The German philosopher certainly was one of the choice spirits not only of his time, but of all time.

The various projects which have been outlined in passing, without entering into their details, made but a limited appeal; they made little or no impression upon the public at large. They contemplated changes in the society of nations which would either have sacrificed or jeopardized the independence of nations. They disregarded systematically the equality of nations. For the most part they advocated either a perpetual and forcible union, or at least a voluntary federation, and they required for their operation a change of thought as well as a change in the standard of conduct. They were opposed to existing conditions, and for that reason they lacked a substantial basis on which to rear permanent structures. Mr. Ladd, on the contrary, accepted nations as actually constituted, proposed a Congress of such nations, in which each would be represented with an equal vote, and the establishment of a court of justice for the settlement of disputes between them. Living in a free country where public opinion is controlled by the people as a whole, he realized the necessity of following public opinion, and the spirit of his project was that an educated public opinion might in time force itself upon the government of its choice. Interesting in itself, Ladd's project deserves examination and consideration by reason of its prophecy

* Kant, *Zum ewigen Frieden* (*Sämmtliche Werke*); loc. cit., pt. 7, p. 291; Wheaton, op. cit., p. 753.

of a conference, and may not be dismissed with a mere mention. The various projects which have been mentioned were drafted by Europeans and had particular reference to European conditions and institutions insofar as actual conditions were considered or referred to.   Mr. Ladd's plan betrays its American origin, although he himself refers to and relies upon Swiss experience and institutions, substituting an international for a national congress and an international for a supreme court.

Mr. Ladd's plan for the establishment of a Congress to make international law and a court to interpret and apply it is found in his *Essay on a Congress of Nations*, published in Boston in the year 1840, and it is not too much to say that this little book contained within its covers, and within singularly narrow compass, not merely the arguments for, but the arguments against the establishment of both institutions.

The plan consisted of two parts:

> 1st.   A congress of ambassadors from all those Christian and civilized nations who should choose to send them, for the purpose of settling the principles of international law by compact and agreement, of the nature of a mutual treaty, and also of devising and promoting plans for the preservation of peace, and meliorating the condition of man.
> 2d.   A court of nations, composed of the most able civilians in the world, to arbitrate or judge such cases as should be brought before it, by the mutual consent of two or more contending nations.*

Upon this firm foundation Mr. Ladd rests his structure, which will one day take visible form in a stated periodic conference of the nations at The Hague and in an international court of justice, likewise at The Hague.

For the details and elaboration necessary for a correct understanding of the nature and the rôle each institution was destined to play in the economy of nations, we might refer to Mr. Ladd's *Essay* without further description, analysis, or quotation, and yet so to do would be unfair to Mr. Ladd, whose main principles should be here stated as far as possible in his own words, in order that his

---

* Advertisement, post, p. xlix.

project might be compared with the classic projects already mentioned, and in order that the reader might see its relation to the international movement which began with the Czar's manifesto for an international conference at The Hague. The material portion of Mr. Ladd's views, both as to the Congress and as to the Court of Nations, are therefore set out in his own words in this place.

First, as to the congress of nations:

1. Our plan is composed of two parts, viz., a Congress of Nations and a Court of Nations, either of which might exist without the other, but they would tend much more to the happiness of mankind if united in one plan, though not in one body. A congress of ambassadors from all those Christian and civilized nations who should choose to unite in the measure, is highly desirable to fix the fluctuating and various points of international law, by the consent of all the parties represented, making the law of nations so plain that a court composed of the most eminent jurists of the countries represented at the Congress, could easily apply those principles to any particular case brought before them. Such a congress would provide for the organization of such a court; but they would not constitute that court; which would be permanent, like the Supreme Court of the United States, while the Congress would be transient or periodical, with a change of members like the Congress or Senate of the United States. It is not proposed that the legislative and judiciary bodies shall be united. The Congress of Nations, therefore, is one body, and the creator of the Court of Nations, which is another distinct body. Any nation represented at the Congress might change its delegates as often as it pleased, like other ambassadors, but the members of the court would hold their offices during good behavior.

2. The Congress of Nations would be organized by a convention, composed of ambassadors from all those Christian or civilized nations who should concur in the measure, each nation having one vote, however numerous may be the ambassadors sent to the convention. . . .

3. After organization, the Congress would proceed to the consideration of the first principles of the law of nations as they are laid down by civilians and agreed to by treaties, throwing all the light which the congregated wisdom of the civilized world contains on the principles of international law, and applying those principles to classes of individual cases. No principle would be established, unless it had the unanimous

consent of all the nations represented at the Congress, and ratified by all the governments of those nations, so that each and every principle would resemble a treaty, by which each nation represented bound itself to every other nation represented, to abide by certain expressed principles in their future intercourse with one another; which agreement or treaty shall not be annulled, except by the consent of all the parties making it.

4. That the progress of such a Congress would be very slow, it must be allowed; but so far from being the worse, it would be the better for that, and more likely to produce permanent and useful results. It would not be necessary that each article of the compact, thus entered into, should be ratified by the nations concerned, before the Congress proceeded to settle other points; but the whole, having been agreed on in Congress, could be submitted to the governments represented, and such points as should be unanimously adopted should be considered as settled points of international law, and the remainder left open for further investigation; and thus all the most material points of international law would be forever settled, and other points put in a fair way of being settled. The Court of Nations need not be delayed until all the points of international law were settled; but its organization might be one of the first things for the Congress of Nations to do, and in the mean time, the Court of Nations might decide cases brought before it on principles generally known and acknowledged.*

Next, as to the court of nations:

1. It is proposed to organize a Court of Nations, composed of as many members as the Congress of Nations shall previously agree upon, say two from each of the powers represented at the Congress. The power of the court to be merely advisory. It is to act as a high court of admiralty, but without its enforcing powers. There is to be no sheriff, or posse, to enforce its commands. It is to take cognizance only of such cases as shall be referred to it, by the free and mutual consent of both parties concerned, like a chamber of commerce; and is to have no more power to enforce its decisions than an ecclesiastical court in this country.

2. The members of this court are to be appointed by the governments represented in the Congress of Nations, and shall hold their places according to the tenure previously agreed on in the Congress—probably during good behavior. Whether

* Post, pp. 8-10.

they should be paid by the governments sending them, or by the nations represented in the Congress conjointly, according to the ratio of their population or wealth, may be agreed on in the Congress. The court should organize itself by choosing a president and vice-presidents from among themselves, and appoint the necessary clerks, secretaries, reporters, etc.; and they should hear counsel on both sides of the questions to be judged. They might meet once a year for the transaction of business, and adjourn to such time and place as they should think proper. Their meeting should never be in a country which had a case on trial. These persons should enjoy the same privileges and immunities as ambassadors.

3. Their verdicts, like the verdicts of other great courts, should be decided by a majority, and need not be, like the decrees of the Congress, unanimous. . . .

4. All cases submitted to the court should be judged by the true interpretation of existing treaties, and by the laws enacted by the Congress and ratified by the nations represented; and where these treaties and laws fail of establishing the point at issue, they should judge the cause by the principles of equity and justice.

5. In cases of disputed boundary, the court should have the power to send surveyors appointed by themselves, but at the expense of the parties, to survey the boundaries, collect facts on the spot, and report to the court. . . .

6. This court should not only decide on all cases brought before it by any two or more independent, contending nations, but they should be authorized to offer their mediation where war actually exists, or in any difficulty arising between any two or more nations which would endanger the peace of the world. . . .

8. It should be the duty of a Court of Nations, from time to time, to suggest topics for the consideration of the Congress, as new or unsettled principles, favorable to the peace and welfare of nations, would present themselves to the court, in the adjudication of cases. . . .

9. There are many other cases beside those above mentioned, in which such a court would either prevent war or end it. A nation would not be justified, in the opinion of the world, in going to war, when there was an able and impartial umpire to judge its case; and many a dispute would be quashed at the outset, if it were known that the world would require an impartial investigation of it by able judges.*

* Post, pp. 34-7.

Mr. Ladd, it will be recalled, regarded the congress as a diplomatic body and the court as a judicial body, and the only credit he takes to himself is for their separation. The line of separation, however, is on one occasion blurred or indistinctly drawn, as he allows the members of the court " to offer their mediation where war actually exists or in any difficulty arising between any two or more nations which would endanger the peace of the world." It would seem that providing the court with powers of mediation testifies to the goodness of his heart rather than to the strength of his understanding, for mediation is political, therefore diplomatic. It can hardly be called a judicial function. The matter, however, is trifling, and is mentioned as perhaps the chief if not the sole instance in which Mr. Ladd disregarded the separation of functions of the two international agencies.

In the following passage Mr. Ladd outlines at once the policy of his Congress and the actual program of the Hague Conferences:

> The Congress of Nations is to have nothing to do with the internal affairs of nations, or with insurrections, revolutions, or contending factions of people or princes, or with forms of government, but solely to concern themselves with the intercourse of nations in peace and war. 1st. To define the rights of belligerents towards each other; and endeavor, as much as possible, to abate the horrors of war, lessen its frequency, and promote its termination. 2d. To settle the rights of neutrals, and thus abate the evils which war inflicts on those nations that are desirous of remaining in peace. 3d. To agree on measures of utility to mankind in a state of peace; and 4th, To organize a Court of Nations. Those are the four great divisions of the labors of the proposed Congress of Nations.*

The resemblance between Ladd's project and the Hague Conferences is so patent as to need no comment, and while it would be an exaggeration to insist that the Conference is the direct result of Ladd's *Essay on a Congress of Nations,* it would be unfair not to state that Ladd's project became widely known in America, where public opinion was created in its behalf; that it was published in England, and influenced the peace movement along Ladd's lines, and that the project for the establishment of a Congress and a

* Post, p. 10.

Court of Nations was, by the faithful disciple, Elihu Burritt, laid before the various Peace Conferences of Brussels (1848), Paris (1849), Frankfort (1850), and London (1851).

It is perhaps not too much to say that had not the Crimean War broken out in the fifties, the experiment of a conference would have been tried and a permanent court established long before the present generation.

In commenting upon Saint-Pierre's scheme, Cardinal Fleury pleasantly told the author of the *Essay* that " he had forgotten one preliminary article, which was the delegation of missionaries to dispose the hearts of the princes of Europe to submit to such a diet." To which Ladd replied:

> The peace societies must furnish these missionaries, and send them to the princes in monarchial governments, and to the people in mixed and republican governments. Let public opinion be on our side, and missionaries will not be wanting.*

And again:

> Before either the President or the Congress of these United States will act on this subject, the sovereign people must act, and before they will act, they must be acted on by the friends of peace; and the subject must be laid before the people, in all parts of our country, as much as it has been in Massachusetts, where there has, probably, been as much said and done on the subject, as in all the other twenty-five states of the Union. When the whole country shall understand the subject as well as the state of Massachusetts, the Congress of the United States will be as favorable to a Congress of Nations as the General Court of Massachusetts; and when the American Government shall take up the subject in earnest, it will begin to be studied and understood by the enlightened nations of Europe.†

Mr. Ladd cherished no illusions. He believed that his plan was practical, and believing, likewise, that it was wise and just, he felt that it could wait years, if need be, for its realization, and that repeated failures would not prevent ultimate triumph. For example, after describing various attempts to form a Congress of Nations, especially at Panama, he says:

* Post, p. 62.

† Post, p. 72.

The inference to be deduced from this abortive attempt [at Panama] is, that the governments of Christendom are willing to send delegates to any such Congress, whenever it shall be called *by a respectable state,* well established in its own government, if called in a time of peace, to meet at a proper place. That this attempt at a Congress of Nations, or even a dozen more, should prove abortive on account of defects in their machinery or materials, ought not to discourage us, any more than the dozen incipient attempts at a steamboat, which proved abortive for similar reasons, should have discouraged Fulton. Every failure throws new light on this subject, which is founded in the principles of truth and equity. Some monarch, president, or statesman—some moral Fulton, as great in ethics as he was in physics, will yet arise, and complete this great moral machine, so as to make it practically useful, but improvable by coming generations. Before the fame of such a man, your Caesars, Alexanders, and Napoleons will hide their diminished heads, as the twinkling stars of night fade away before the glory of the full-orbed king of day.*

When the Conference called by the " respectable state ", namely, Russia, shall have become permanent and assemble periodically to correct the inequalities and deficiencies of the law of nations, and when a court of nations composed of judges exists as a permanent institution before which nations appear as suitors, and when mankind, accustomed to these institutions, recognize their importance, the name of William Ladd will undoubtedly figure among the benefactors of his kind.

JAMES BROWN SCOTT,
Director of the Division of International Law.

WASHINGTON, D. C.,
February 28, 1916.

* Post, p. 57.

CONTENTS

CONTENTS

ADVERTISEMENT.

As this Essay is expected to go out to the world as a separate pamphlet, or volume, as well as to be bound up with the Prize Essays on a Congress of Nations, published by the American Peace Society, it is necessary to notify those to whom it may come separate of this circumstance. Thirty-five of the dissertations, out of a greater number—I believe about forty—which were handed in for the purpose of claiming the reward offered by two gentlemen of New York, through the American Peace Society, have been read by me. Others have been withdrawn, some of which have been published by the authors of them. The Society concluded to accept the advice of the first committee of award,—the Hon. Messrs. Story, Wirt and Calhoun,—to publish the five best Essays; as the second committee, consisting of Ex-president Adams, Chancellor Kent and the Hon. Daniel Webster, did not agree on the successful competitor. The Peace Society appointed a committee of their own body to select five of the best dissertations for publication, having an eye to the awards of the abovenamed committees, and directed me to add a sixth, taking all the matter from the rejected Essays worth preserving, which is not contained in the Essays selected for publication. I have attended to this duty. In reading over these Essays, I noted down every thought worth preserving; and I present them here in a body, with such reflections, additions and historical facts as occurred to me during my labor; so that my claim to originality, in this production, rests much on the thought of separating the subject into two distinct parts, viz., 1st. A congress of ambassadors from all those Christian and civilized nations who should choose to send them, for the purpose of settling the principles of international law by compact and agreement, of the nature of a mutual treaty, and also of devising and promoting plans for the preservation of peace, and meliorating the condition of man. 2d. A court of nations, composed of the most able civilians in the world, to arbitrate or judge such cases as should be brought before

ADVERTISEMENT

it, by the mutual consent of two or more contending nations: thus dividing entirely the diplomatic from the judicial functions, which require such different, not to say opposite, characters in the exercise of their functions. I consider the Congress as the legislature, and the Court as the judiciary, in the government of nations, leaving the functions of the executive with public opinion, " the queen of the world." This division I have never seen in any essay or plan for a congress or diet of independent nations, either ancient or modern; and I believe it will obviate all the objections which have been heretofore made to such a plan.

I advise all persons, into whose hand this Essay may fall, to purchase the volume of Prize Essays, published by the American Peace Society, for they will find them, in many respects, very far superior to this in style and richness of matter, both historical and original; and they will also assist the Society, now burthened with debt, which will be increased by the publication of these Essays, unless they meet with a ready sale.

WILLIAM LADD.

BOSTON, FEBRUARY, 1840.

ESSAY.

*CHAPTER I.

INTRODUCTION AND GENERAL REMARKS.

1. SELF-LOVE is a passion universally predominant in the animal, man. It was born with him, is inherent in his nature, and is the mainspring of all his actions, while he continues in his natural state. In this state, man seeks the gratification of his animal passions, without regard to the welfare of others. As this is the case with every man in a state of nature, it follows, that every man is liable to come into conflict with every other man in his immediate neighborhood, and to resort to violence to gratify his lusts and passions. Hence, as was observed by Hobbes, *6 " the * natural state of man is war," in which the strong and the cunning will always obtain the mastery over the weak and unsuspecting; and will rob, murder, and enslave them, whenever they think it expedient.

2. But man is a social being, and he feels it not good for him to be alone; and he chooses to himself a partner of his joys and sorrows, whom, by force, fraud, or persuasion, he obtains. A family of children is the consequence. The parents are bound to one another, and to their children, by a softer, but as strong, a tie as self-love — or rather it is self-

love extended to their partner and to their children. Hence come families, the germs of nations, bound together by affection to their clan, and governed by patriarchal authority, until they find it convenient or necessary to part, and each individual becomes the germ of a new family, tribe, or nation.

3. But man is also a rational animal, and he soon perceives that there are enjoyments which can more easily be procured by persuasion, than by force; and that though he may be stronger than another individual, two other individuals may be stronger than he — that he cannot always be on the watch to preserve the property he has acquired by robbery, the chase, or agriculture — and that he also is subject to inconvenience from the theft, or violence, of others; hence he soon finds himself compelled to make a certain convention, or agreement, with others, both inferiors and equals, both as an individual and as the head of a tribe. These compacts are guaranteed by religion, public opinion, and certain undefined laws of honor * dependent on them; but most of all by a general perception of the truth, that the happiness of the whole is best promoted by the subservience of the interests of the few to the interests of the many.

* 7

4. It would be pleasing to the philanthropist, if he could conceive that the ways abovementioned were the only ones in which states have been formed; but, unhappily, it is not so. From the first ages, Nimrods, mighty men of war, by force or fraud, have enslaved other men, held them in bondage and vassalage, and been obliged to make laws for them, which have continued, with more or less severity, until those slaves and vassals have become more enlightened, and taken a part, or the whole, of the government into their own hands.

5. In some few cases, the people, feeling their incompetency to govern themselves, have been willing to continue under the paternal government of the elder branch of the family, and hereditary monarchy, at times accompanied with a change in the reigning family, has followed. Under these various forms of government, man has been infinitely happier, than he would have been in a state of nature and anarchy; and generally nations have, naturally and without consultation, taken that form of government best adapted to the people. For many nations, absolute monarchy is best, for some a limited monarchy, for a few a republican form, and for a few very small states, even a pure democracy is perhaps the best; but the different features of all these forms of government are variously combined in infinite diversity, according to the genius of the people governed.

* 8   * 6. The chief end and purpose of government is, to prevent one person from injuring another; so that every one may sit under his own vine and fig-tree, with none to molest or make him afraid. This is the object of all our laws, and all the expensive machinery of government, which has taken care that no individual should molest his neighbor; and when disputes arise, so far from leaving each individual to take his cause into his own hands, governments have provided courts of law to decide the controversy. In many governments, the legislative has been entirely separated from the judicial power, and the executive from both. In all of them, the impartiality of the judicial power has been in a ratio equal to the knowledge and virtue of the people. In some of these governments, laws have been made, not only for securing the rights of private individuals, but also of bodies corporate, and even of component parts of the empire which are for many purposes independent. No

such thing has yet been done with respect to nations, though courts have been instituted, to decide controversies which have arisen between two or more members of the same confederacy of nations. Our object is to go one step further, and appoint a court, by which contests between nations shall be settled, without resort to arms, when any such controversy shall be brought, by mutual consent, before it.

7. By consent of all writers on international law, nations are considered as individual, moral persons, perfectly equal and independent of one another. Therefore, the *9   same moral laws which ought to govern * individuals, ought to govern nations. What is wrong for an individual, is wrong for a nation. In the intercourse of these moral persons, disputes will arise, injuries will be done, retaliation and revenge will follow, and, unless some means of terminating their disputes by amicable and rational methods are devised, war will be the consequence. There are three ways already in use, whereby war may be avoided. The first is, by cultivating a spirit of peace, which is the spirit of the gospel, and is as much the duty of nations as it is of individuals; by this means, injuries, especially if not very grievous, will be overlooked, or be passed by with a bare remonstrance, and an appeal to the moral sense of the nation that has inflicted the injury. The second is, by negotiation, where the subject in dispute is formally discussed and settled by reparation or compromise. If this cannot be done, the next step is mediation of a friendly power, accompanied with arbitration and the acceptance of the award. The last resort is war, which commonly increases, instead of remedying the evil. We propose a plan more likely to procure justice than either of these.

8. As government is an ordinance of God, necessary for the safety, happiness and improvement of the human race, and as it is absolutely necessary for the peace of society, that when the selfish passions of man come in conflict, the judgment of the case should not be left with the individuals concerned, but with some impartial tribunal; so it is

* 10   equally necessary, for the peace and happiness of mankind, that when the * selfish passions of *nations*

come in conflict, the decision of the case should not be left with an individual nation concerned, but should be referred to some great tribunal, that should give a verdict on the affairs of nations, in the same manner that a civil court decides the disputes of individuals. If it was desirable for individuals, bodies politic, and small independent tribes, to unite in some general system of jurisprudence, why is it not equally desirable for large tribes and nations to do the same?

9. There are two difficulties in the way, which require our attention; but it will be found that they may as easily be removed as were the difficulties attending the commencement and advancement of institutions for the adjudication of difficulties arising between individuals. The first of these is the want of a body of men to enact and promulgate laws for the government of nations; the other is the want of a physical force to carry the decisions of a court of nations into execution.

10. As to the first difficulty, the formation of what we call a CONGRESS OF NATIONS is no greater than the assembling of any convention for the enactment of laws, by mutual consent, for the government of the parties represented. It is not expected, that such a combination of powers would be of a very great geographical extent, as it could only embrace the most civilized, enlightened, and Christian

nations that could be represented at one great diet, by their ambassadors; and there form a league and covenant,

* 11   each with every one, and every one with each, that * they would, in their future intercourse, be governed by the laws enacted by the diet or congress and ratified by the governments of all the powers so represented. The world has now a kind of code of *voluntary* international law, laid down by eminent civilians, which is, for the most part, respected, but which is not confirmed, by any compact or agreement, and on which the authors themselves often differ, so that what is now called the law of nations, is but little better than a nose of wax, which may be twisted either way, to suit the purposes of dominant nations.

11. The magnitude of the second difficulty is apparently greater, but it will be much reduced by reflection. It is true, it would not comport with the peace and happiness of mankind, to invest rulers with the power to compel an acquiescence in the decisions of a COURT OF NATIONS by arms; but if we look into the condition of man in a state of civilization, it will be found, that where one man obeys the laws for fear of the sword of the magistrate, an hundred obey them through fear of public opinion. But I would further observe, 1st, that public opinion has not yet been made to bear on nations, and little or no means have hitherto been used to make it bear on them. The plan we propose is one of the means eminently adapted to make it bear on them, as will be shown in the sequel. 2. We do not know what means the congregated wisdom of Christendom may devise for the enforcement of the decisions of a court of nations, by so regulating the intercourse of nations that a

* 12   refractory member might be made to feel that its duty * is its true interest. 3. As it is not intended that this court of nations shall judge any cases but such as are submitted to it by the mutual consent of both parties concerned, its decisions will have as much to enforce them as the decisions of an individual umpire, which has so often settled disputes between nations. 4. Though at the commencement of this system, its success may not be so great as is desirable, yet, as moral power is every day increasing in a geometrical ratio, it will finally take the place of all wars between civilized and Christian nations, much in the same manner as a civil court has taken the place of the judicial combat. With these preliminaries we now proceed to a more minute consideration of a Congress and a Court of Nations, each by itself.

*CHAPTER II.

ON THE ORGANIZATION OF THE PROPOSED CONGRESS OF NATIONS.

1. A Congress of Nations a separate thing from a Court of Nations—2. Organization of the Congress—3. Formation of a Code of International Law—4. Progress necessarily slow—5. No concern with internal affairs of Nations.

1. OUR plan is composed of two parts, viz., a Congress of Nations and a Court of Nations, either of which might exist without the other, but they would tend much more to the happiness of mankind if united in one plan, though not in one body. A congress of ambassadors from all those Christian and civilized nations who should choose to unite in the measure, is highly desirable to fix the fluctuating and various points of international law, by the consent of all the parties represented, making the law of nations so plain that a court composed of the most eminent jurists of the countries represented at the Congress, could easily apply those principles to any particular case brought before them. Such a congress would provide for the organization of such a court; but they would not constitute that court; which would be permanent, like the Supreme Court of the United States, while the Congress would be transient or periodical, with a change of members like the Congress or Senate of the United States. It is not proposed that the legis- * 14 lative and judiciary bodies shall be * united. The Congress of Nations, therefore, is one body, and the creator of the Court of Nations, which is another distinct body. Any nation represented at the Congress might

8

change its delegates as often as it pleased, like other ambassadors, but the members of the court would hold their offices during good behaviour.

2. The Congress of Nations would be organized by a convention, composed of ambassadors from all those Christian or civilized nations who should concur in the measure, each nation having one vote, however numerous may be the ambassadors sent to the convention. This convention would organize themselves into a Congress of Nations, by adopting such regulations and by-laws as might appear expedient to the majority. Those who would not agree with the majority would, of course, have leave to withdraw from the convention, which would then constitute the Congress of Nations, choose its president, vice-presidents, secretaries, clerks, and such other officers as they would see fit. New members might be received, at any time subsequent to the first organization of the Congress, by their embracing the rules already adopted and the nations sending them adopting the laws of nations enacted by the Congress, and duly ratified before their becoming members of the confederation.

3. After organization, the Congress would proceed to the consideration of the first principles of the law of nations as they are laid down by civilians and agreed to by
* 15 treaties, throwing all the light which the * congregated wisdom of the civilized world contains on the principles of international law, and applying those principles to classes of individual cases. No principle would be established, unless it had the unanimous consent of all the nations represented at the Congress, and ratified by all the governments of those nations, so that each and every principle would resemble a treaty, by which each nation represented bound itself to every other nation represented, to abide by

certain expressed principles in their future intercourse with one another; which agreement or treaty shall not be annulled, except by the consent of all the parties making it.

4. That the progress of such a Congress would be very slow, it must be allowed; but so far from being the worse, it would be the better for that, and more likely to produce permanent and useful results. It would not be necessary that each article of the compact, thus entered into, should be ratified by the nations concerned, before the Congress proceeded to settle other points; but the whole, having been agreed on in Congress, could be submitted to the governments represented, and such points as should be unanimously adopted should be considered as settled points of international law, and the remainder left open for further investigation; and thus all the most material points of international law would be for ever settled, and other points put in a fair way of being settled. The Court of Nations need not be delayed until all the points of international law were settled; but its organization might be one of the
* 16   first * things for the Congress of Nations to do, and in the mean time, the Court of Nations might decide cases brought before it on principles generally known and acknowledged.

5. The Congress of Nations is to have nothing to do with the internal affairs of nations, or with insurrections, revolutions, or contending factions of people or princes, or with forms of government, but solely to concern themselves with the intercourse of nations in peace and war. 1st. To define the rights of belligerents towards each other; and endeavor, as much as possible, to abate the horrors of war, lessen its frequency, and promote its termination. 2d. To settle the rights of neutrals, and thus abate the evils which

war inflicts on those nations that are desirous of remaining in peace. 3d. To agree on measures of utility to mankind in a state of peace; and 4th, To organize a Court of Nations. These are the four great divisions of the labors of the proposed Congress of Nations.

*CHAPTER III.

ON THE RIGHTS OF BELLIGERENTS WITH RESPECT TO EACH OTHER.

1. The rights of belligerents have their limits—2. The right to declare war—3. Are all means of destroying an enemy lawful?—4. Confiscation of private debts—5. Detention of the subjects of an enemy—6. Who may be made prisoners of war?—7. Property liable to capture—8. Voyages of discovery—9. Compacts with an enemy—10. Of Truce—11. Of Retaliation.

1. THE rights of belligerents have their limits, even as they respect one another. Humanity has been shocked and outraged by excesses committed by them; and there is no good reason why nations should not mutually agree to frown on all the cruelties of war which are unnecessary to the ostensible object of it. A nation, by declaring war, makes every subject of the country against whom war is declared, technically speaking, an enemy — *hostis,* a national enemy, not *inimicus,* or a personal enemy. It would be hard to show that the gospel has made any difference; but man has; and a person may be an enemy, according to the law of nations, who is a friend and brother, according to the law of God. If nations will continue to make war, they should endeavor to violate the law of God as little as possible, and put all practicable bounds to savage exhibitions of national enmity. The rights of belligerents over their enemies ought to be regulated by acknowledged

*17   principles; * and the condition of prisoners of war and of the vanquished should be, as much as possible, ameliorated. Vattel holds that prisoners of war may be

made slaves, when we may lawfully kill them.* Burlamaqui
thinks we may kill them in " cases of necessity." † Formerly
prisoners of war were enslaved or put to death without
disgrace, and until a very late date, viz., the wars between
Charles XII of Sweden, and Peter the great, of Russia,
prisoners were made slaves during the war; but the increased
light of Christianity leaves but little to be done on this
subject.

2. The question should be settled by the Congress,
Whether a nation, unless attacked, has a right to declare war
against another nation, or make reprisals, until it has
resorted to all other means of obtaining justice, such as
negotiation, and an offer to leave the dispute to arbitration,
or to cast lots, or settle the dispute by the ordeal of battle
by two or more champions? The last two modes of settling
international difficulties are not seriously proposed in this
age of light and good feeling, but only to show, that, however absurd they are in themselves, they are altogether better for both the parties concerned, and for the
world at large, than the greater absurdity of war, and
just as likely to do justice to the parties, at a much
less expense of life and money. Many other questions
should be solved by the Congress, such as the following:

* 18   * 3. Are all means of destroying an enemy lawful?
Is it lawful to poison an enemy's food, or his springs
and wells of water, — to use poisoned arms, to fire at him
such missiles as broken glass bottles and rusty nails, which
inflict almost incurable wounds, without killing, — to make
use of torpedoes, fireships, mines, &c. Is assassination to be
allowed; and under what circumstances? Burlamaqui
allows of assassination of an enemy under certain circum-

* See his Law of Nations, lib. iii, § 152.   † Burlamaqui, part 3, c. v, § 8.

stances.* He reasons correctly and ingeniously, when he says, " If we may employ a great number of men to kill an enemy, we may certainly employ a less number," though he doubts whether we may employ one of the enemy's subjects to do it by falsehood and treason. But what is employing deserters, but hiring men to kill their compatriots; and what are falsehood and treason, but stratagems of war? It is not morally worse to cut off an enemy by assassination, than by ambuscade, torpedo, or mine, and if I may do it by hiring traitors and deserters in masses, why may I not do it by a single traitor or deserter? How many allow of employing deserters or traitors in masses, who would shudder at the thought of employing a single deserter to do similar things! By beginning to prohibit the employing of single deserters or traitors, Christian nations may, at length, come to prohibit the employment of deserters and traitors in masses.

4. Has a nation, by declaring war, a right to confiscate private debts due from the enemy to its
*20 own * subjects? During the war of the American
revolution, the Americans confiscated the private debts due from American to British subjects; and as a bribe to betray the debts, a part of the spoils was offered to the debtors. This principle was afterward abandoned, and in the treaty of peace, indemnity to the British merchants was promised. Vattel thinks that a belligerent has a right to confiscate such debts, or at least to detain the payment during the war.† A Congress of Nations should settle this question.

5. Has a nation a right, on going to war, to detain the subjects of an enemy, either civil or military, who may happen to be in its territory; and to what extent shall that

* Burlamaqui, part 4, c. vi, § 15.   † Law of Nations, book 3, § 77.

right be exercised? — on the military only, or on civilians also? — on men only, or on women and children also, and on property? On the breaking out of war after the short peace of Amiens, Napoleon detained the British subjects that were found in France, as prisoners of war, but how far he carried this principle, I do not know. His motives probably were to draw money, for their support, from England.

6. Who shall be considered as combatants and liable to be made prisoners of war? Formerly all the subjects of an enemy were considered combatants, and alike liable to be made prisoners of war and to be murdered, or sold into slavery. Civilized society, under the mild influence of Christianity, has much ameliorated the condition of conquered enemies, and but very few, except such as are found *21   with arms in * their hands, are excluded from the list of non-combatants. It is very desirable to extend this list, so as to include the man who catches whales, as well as the man who catches smaller fishes — the man who ploughs the ocean on his own peaceful business, as well as the man who ploughs the field.

7. What property of an enemy shall be liable to capture? Formerly all property, both public and private, real and personal, became the property of the captor. Now, private property on shore is respected, and property afloat only is captured. A merchant vessel, on the stocks, is not liable to capture; on the water she is, except small vessels employed in the fisheries. Cicero observes, that it is not contrary to the law of nations to plunder a person whom we may lawfully kill.* But if we may plunder those only whom we may lawfully kill, then we should no longer plunder the peaceful merchant. May a conqueror seize private landed

* Cicero, De Officiis, lib. 3, c. vi.

estate as the spoils of war? May churches and public property of a civil nature be plundered by an enemy? Burlamaqui allows it; but it has become a reproach to any people to do it. The burning of the capitol at Washington was justified by the British on the plea of retaliation; and even, on this plea, they begin to be ashamed of it.

8. A Congress of Nations might settle what protection should be afforded to the ships of enemies making voyages of discovery. The American government, and, I * 22   believe, the French also, agreed not to * molest the squadron of Captain Cook. Missionary stations, settlements on barbarous coasts for benevolent purposes, light-houses, buoys, beacons, and even the military hospitals of the enemy, should be respected.

9. Is a compact made with an enemy at an end as soon as war is declared? Grotius is of opinion that contracts made with an enemy are binding. Puffendorf doubts it.

10. What is the nature of a truce? and what formalities are necessary at its commencement and its end? What rights does a belligerent give up by a truce? and what does he retain? What rights belong to heralds, flags of truce and cartels? How may intercourse be carried on between belligerents? What security does a safe conduct concede? What is the nature of parole, ransom, and the giving of hostages? Even in this day of comparative light, it may be well to put some limits to the right which a belligerent has over the person of his enemy by the general consent and treaty stipulations of all Christian nations, each being bound to all; and a Congress of Nations is the only place where such a compact can be executed.

11. Cannot something be done to meliorate the barbarous custom of retortion and retaliation; or at least to regulate it? How are spies, deserters, and prisoners who have

violated their parole to be treated? Is it not possible to
put some limit to the power of a belligerent over the
* 23   life of his enemy? Is it allowable, * under any
circumstances, to kill unresisting persons, who have
been guilty of no offence but being made enemies by
proclamation? There is reason to hope, that much may be
done to moderate the severity of war in all these particulars,
in a body representing the congregated wisdom of Christendom; and as the judicial combat gradually gave place to
the grand assize, when the follies and cruelties of the ordeal
by battle were exposed and mitigated, so the ordeal of war
may gradually give place to a court of nations.

*CHAPTER IV.

ON CERTAIN RIGHTS OF BELLIGERENTS WHICH MAY AFFECT NEUTRALS ALSO.

1. The rights of conquest—2. Of Expatriation—3. Privateering—4. Neutrals found in an enemy's camp.

1. UNDER this head there is one very important question to be settled by a Congress of Nations, viz., How long shall a territory remain in possession of the conqueror before it shall be considered as his own, so that he may convey it away to another nation, and for ever cut off the right of the former owner? One would naturally suppose, that when a treaty of peace is ratified, ceding the conquered or disputed territory, the right of the former possessor would for ever cease; but this doctrine is disputed, and some Americans have hinted at a claim to the western coast of North America, on the ground that its relinquishment to England by Spain, was the effect of compulsion; and that since the purchase of Louisiana and all which belonged to it, we stand in the place of Spain with respect to the north-west coast of America, and have a right to claim it, as soon as we are strong enough. We ought, however, to remember, that the cession of Louisiana to France, from whom we bought it, was also the effect of compulsion, and Spain would have an equal right to reclaim the whole * 25 from us. * The American forces in Georgia were authorized by government to receive Amelia Island in East Florida from whomever should be in possession of it. If we had received Texas into our Union, would it have

18

been consistent with the existing law of nations? The principles on which such things should be regulated, can only be settled by a Congress of Nations.

2. It is highly important to the peace of the world in general, and of Great Britain and the United States of America in particular, that the right of expatriation should be better understood than it is now. The American government claims the right of naturalizing foreigners in such a manner as to affect their allegiance to their native country. During the late wars in Europe, it was stated by a committee of the Congress of the United States, that 6257 Americans had been impressed into the navy of Great Britain; but what proportion of them were natives of that power, naturalized here, the committee do not state. The subject of impressment was the principal cause of the last war between Great Britain and America, though Great Britain had always disclaimed the right of impressing native Americans. Before another war breaks out in Europe, this principle of expatriation should be settled. Some may think that this article would come better in the next chapter; but though the settlement of this question is of great importance with respect to neutrals generally, and to Great Britain and America in particular; to all the rest of the world, it is of great importance as it respects belligerents also.

Certainly a nation has a natural right to deal with her * 26 own subjects * as she may think proper, and a Congress or Court of Nations would not interfere; but the great question is, Who are her own subjects? In settling this question, the United States are at variance with almost all the rest of the world, and the settlement of the question, — whether a man has a right to expatriate himself or not, — is of great importance to us, not only as a neutral, but as a belligerent. Having a great number of naturalized foreigners among us, and our army being composed, in a great measure, of such characters, it is important for us to know whether we ought to retaliate, if any of them, taken fighting against their native country, should be condemned to death, and whether, by the present law of nations and general usage, we should have a right to put to death Americans only, taken in arms against this country, or any other prisoners of war also. These important questions can never be settled by any unauthorized writers on the law of nations, and can only be done by a compact and agreement. I think that Great Britain would be willing to relinquish her assumed right of searching our ships for her seamen on the high seas, — and perhaps in her own waters also, — for the right of searching for slaves under our flag on the coast of Africa, which right we now deny.

3. A Congress of Nations could settle the great question, so long agitated, whether privateering should any longer be allowed in carrying on the wars of civilized and Christian countries; and this relic of barbarism and piracy be at last done away. The government of the United States *27 has made great * endeavors to abolish this evil, though with but little success. The instructions given, by the Congress of the old confederation, to our ambassadors abroad, directed them to endeavor to procure the general abolition of the practice of privateering. Frederick III of Prussia was the only one who consented to give up the practice; but in a Congress of Nations its entire abolition would easily be effected.

4. Another question, nearly related to the last two is, the manner in which a belligerent nation may treat the subject of a neutral nation, when found in an enemy's camp, fleet, or privateer? By many, they are considered pirates, and, morally speaking, certainly they are no better. In the same

connection, might be agitated the question, whether, when a nation has offered to leave its disputes with another nation to the Court of Nations, and that other nation shall refuse, or having so referred it, shall refuse to abide by the decision, but should go to war — in such a case, may the subjects of a neutral nation engage in war against the party so offending? If it were ever justifiable to take a part in foreign wars, it would be under such circumstances, and a nation might then allow its subjects to engage in a foreign war, according to the law of nations, if not according to the law of God.

*CHAPTER V.

ON THE RIGHTS OF NEUTRALS, TO BE ESTABLISHED BY THE CONGRESS OF NATIONS.

1. Wars often extend to neutrals—2. Rights of a neutral flag—3. Neutral flag covering enemy's property—4. Salvage on a neutral ship—5. Medicines to a blockaded port—6. Of blockade—7. Of contraband of war—8. Right of search—9. Rights of a belligerent over the crew of a neutral—10. When has a neutral the right to buy captured goods—11. Neutral transports—12. Trade of a neutral in the manufactures of an enemy—13. Neutral trade which is prohibited in time of peace—14. Right of transition through a neutral country—15. Rights of a private neutral to engage in war—16. The right of a nation or an individual to take part in foreign revolutions—17. Extent of neutral rights from the shore—18. Other subjects.

1. WE have considered the rights which the common consent of mankind has allowed to belligerents, in their conduct to each other; but this consent is far from being universal, and many points remain to be settled by the concentration of public opinion in a Congress of Nations. We now come to consider the rights which public opinion has generally given to neutrals, on many points on which there is yet a considerable difference of opinion, not only in the world at large, but also among the writers on international law. It is owing to this uncertainty, that when two powerful nations go to war with one another, almost all the nations of Christendom are, sooner or later, forced into the contest. If the rights of neutrals were better understood — especially if the general
*29   principles, * which should regulate the conduct of neutrals to belligerents and of belligerents to neutrals, were solemnly agreed to by the principal powers of Christendom, assembled in a Congress, — and still more

especially, if there were a high court or congress, to which injured nations might appeal for redress, wars would not spread as they have done, and would not be of long continuance. Some of the questions relative to the rights of neutrals, which might be for ever settled by the Congress of Nations proposed, are as follows:

2. Shall a neutral flag cover all that sails under it, provided the voyage be made from one neutral port to another? The law of nature would seem to demand this. The sea is the highway of nations, and a ship is but an extension of the territory of the nation to which it belongs, especially on the high seas, and until it comes within the territorial jurisdiction of another nation. Hence it would appear, that a belligerent has no more right to impede his enemy in his progress from one neutral nation to another, on board a neutral ship, than he has to impede him in passing from one part of a neutral country to another, especially if this enemy be not a military man. Perhaps some concession to the rights of humanity on this subject might be obtained from a Congress of Nations.

3. Shall a neutral flag cover an enemy's property or person, when bound from a neutral to a belligerent country, and if not, what shall be the law of capture and detention?

Shall freight be paid on an enemy's goods taken out?

* 30 Shall this enemy's * property affect the neutral ship and the rest of the cargo? Burlamaqui is of opinion that neutral vessels, having enemies' property on board, are lawful prize, if such property be on board with the consent of the owners. As to all those questions, he observes, that, "prudence and just policy require that sovereigns should come to some agreement among themselves, in order to avoid the disputes which may arise from these different causes." *

* Burlamaqui's Principles of Natural and Political Law, part 4, c. iv, § 24.

This is the very thing which we are aiming at, in proposing and advocating a Congress of Nations.

4. Under what circumstances shall a neutral ship pay salvage to the belligerent who recaptures her from his enemy? Must the neutral have been carried *infra præsidia* of the captor — or have been twenty-four hours in his possession, and be loaded, in whole or in part, with the property of his enemy? It is hard to make a neutral pay salvage, when he would have been released if he had been carried into the port of the captor.

5. If a pestilence should break out in a blockaded port, would a neutral be allowed to carry medicines to it? Humanity would say, yes. I do not know what a Congress of Nations would say.

6. What shall constitute a blockade? Civilians are not agreed on this subject. Some hold that a port, to be * 31   blockaded, must be invested by sea and * land. Others hold a blockade to be lawful, if the harbor only be guarded by a blockading squadron. What notice shall be given of the blockade? Is it sufficient that a blockade be published by proclamation, and neutral nations warned through their ministers at the court of the blockading power? Or shall a neutral ship be warned once, at least, and within a certain distance of the blockaded port, and her papers endorsed, before she shall be liable to capture for breach of blockade? If a storm drive away the blockading squadron, does the blockade continue in their absence? and shall a ship which enters the blockaded port without warning, be liable to be seized and condemned on her coming out? Shall a neutral ship, which enters a belligerent port before a blockade, be allowed to depart? The " Orders in Council " and the " Berlin and Milan Decrees " were infringements on the ancient law of blockade. Uncertainty on this subject

is a fruitful source of war and enmity. If the whole subject could not be made clear by a Congress of Nations, some of the plainest principles might be settled, and an approximation might be made to a clear understanding and general agreement on the whole subject.

7. It is highly important that the list of articles considered contraband of war should be more clearly defined than it is now, and considerably reduced. Every article of contraband of war should be specified, and not left to general rules. Tar, pitch, hemp, flax, iron, and other * 32 articles used to construct and fit out * men-of-war, are not solely or principally used for that purpose, and should not, in their raw state, be included in the list of articles considered contraband of war; while saltpetre, sulphur, and some other crude articles, are almost wholly used for the purposes of war. But it is of greater importance to have the articles considered contraband of war clearly defined, than the bare extension or curtailment of the list of contraband articles. It is of the utmost importance to a neutral merchant, sending his ship to sea loaded, in whole or in part, with tar, iron, hemp, or flax, to know whether he can ensure his ship as free from contraband of war. Uncertainty on this point not only disturbs the harmony of nations, but may be the cause of endless lawsuits between merchants of the same country — the insurer and insured. It is impossible for any writer on the law of nations to specify what articles shall be considered contraband of war. That can only be done by a Congress of Nations; and if done, it would dry up a fruitful source of war.

8. The right of searching neutral ships for contraband of war and enemies' property has never yet been clearly understood, in all its bearings. Shall the contraband articles, and the property of an enemy alone, be liable to confiscation?

or shall the smallest quantity of naval stores or enemies' property authorize the confiscation of the other part of the cargo and the ship? May a neutral ship be carried into the territory of a belligerent for search, or shall it be done at sea only? Shall freight be paid on the *33 property * seized, or not? These questions can only be settled in a Congress of Nations.

9. Has a belligerent a right to take from a neutral ship, without the consent of her captain, one of the crew who is neither the subject nor the enemy of the belligerent, and thus break the lawful contract of such seaman with the captain? Should it make any difference, if the subject of the enemy had been naturalized in the country of the neutral ship?

10. How long a time shall a captured ship, or goods, remain in the possession of a belligerent, before a neutral has a right to buy them? Grotius thinks not until they are brought within the precincts of the country of the captor. Burlamaqui thinks that the captor has a right to sell them as soon as captured.*

11. Has a neutral ship a right to transport the soldiers and military stores of a belligerent? If not, how shall the crime be punished; and at what time shall the ship, so used, be free from capture and condemnation for the act?

12. Has a belligerent the right to prohibit neutrals from trading in the manufactures of an enemy? Under the " Berlin and Milan Decrees," vessels were condemned for having on board English manufactures, and even for speaking or being boarded by British men-of-war. Were either of these causes of condemnation justifiable by the law of nations?

*34 * 13. Has a neutral a right to carry on a trade in

* See Burlamaqui, part 4, c. vii, § 15, *et seq.*

time of war, which he is not allowed in time of peace? This is a very important question, for on it depends the legality of much of the trade of neutrals. The difficulties attending this question nearly brought the United States into a war with Great Britain, in the early part of the war of the French revolution. American vessels traded directly from French colonies in the West Indies to France, or barely touched at some American port, to neutralize their cargo, without discharging it? This was complained of by the British government, and called out the famous pamphlet entitled " War in Disguise," supposed to have been written under the direction of the English cabinet. On the other hand, the " Navigation Act " of Great Britain was almost entirely suspended, and American vessels were allowed to carry almost any thing to England, from almost any country.

14. Has a belligerent a right to pass through the territory of a neutral without his consent? This is a very difficult and complicated question, and is not likely soon to be settled, even in a Congress of Nations; but some approximation may be made toward a settlement of it. Grotius allows the right, while Burlamaqui denies it, and Vattel allows it in certain cases and denies it in others.*

15. Has a private subject a right to engage in war against a country with which his own country is

* 35 at * peace? It was laid down as a principle by General Jackson, in the case of Arbuthnot and Ambrister, that such characters should be treated as pirates, and this opinion has been sanctioned by the American people. Is this principle a correct one? A Congress of Nations only can settle the question.

16. The right of foreign nations or individuals to take a

* Vattel, book 3, c. vii.

military part in the revolutions of other countries should
be clearly defined, and either allowed or forbidden. Not
only should the right of governments be defined, but the
question should be settled, whether a nation has a right to
allow of forces being raised from among their subjects for
such objects. The world has been much in the dark on this
subject, and contrary opinions have prevailed, according
to circumstances. Great Britain has blamed this country
very severely because we have not prevented our citizens
from taking part in the troubles in Canada; while she has
openly allowed the enlistment of soldiers, to take a part in
the revolutions in Spain and Portugal, and in the American
revolution bought whole regiments of foreign troops. In
1833, two hundred and fifty men were enlisted in England
for the war in Portugal, uncertain which side they would
take.

17. How far from shore shall neutral rights extend?
Some say to the distance of a cannon shot — some to the
distance of a league. Has a belligerent a right to anchor
on a neutral shore, in order to blockade his enemy's fleet
in a neutral harbor? It was very grievous to the
* 36   Americans, during the last great wars * in Europe,
to have British men-of-war anchor off our harbors,
and even in our very roadsteads blockade French ships of
war, and examine every ship going and coming, and impress
seamen. Some of our bays are more than two leagues wide.
Has a belligerent a right to attack an enemy in our bays?

18. There are many other subjects relating to the rights
of neutrals, the principles of which ought to be fixed by
general consent, in a time of peace, while the public mind
is unbiased by passing events; and no power is adequate
to this duty but a Congress of Nations. Were it done, many
wars would be prevented.

*CHAPTER VI.

ON PRINCIPLES AND ACTS OF A CIVIL AND PACIFIC NATURE,
AFFECTING THE INTERCOURSE OF THE WORLD AND THE
HAPPINESS OF MANKIND, TO BE SETTLED AND AGREED
UPON BY A CONGRESS OF NATIONS.

1. The cooperation of nations required for plans of general utility—2. Rights
of ambassadors—3. Surrender of felons and debtors—4. Suppression of the
slave trade and piracy—5. Improvements in international communication—
6. International copy-rights and patents—7. Free navigation of bays and
rivers—8. Rights of discovery and colonization—9. General reduction of
military establishments—10. Restoration of military trophies—11. Other
subjects.

1. THERE are many things of a pacific and civil nature,
which require the cooperation of nations, and which can only
be settled in a congress of ambassadors, where the subjects
may be freely discussed and adjusted.

2. The rights of ambassadors, ministers, envoys, and
consuls, should be settled in such a manner as no longer
to be the subject of international disputes. That the
persons, domestics and property of diplomatic agents should
be exempted from arrest for debt, admits not of a question;
but it is doubtful how far such characters should be exempted
from the operation of the criminal code of the countries
where they reside. I suppose such persons may be
arrested and imprisoned for crime; but I doubt if they
can be further punished in any other way than being
* 38   sent * out of the country or delivered up to their own
government. How far shall an ambassador's house

be an asylum for criminals and debtors, not members of the legation where the crimes were committed, or the debts contracted?

3. The surrender of felons and debtors — Puffendorf is of opinion, that felons should not be delivered up, unless there is a treaty stipulation to that effect. Now a Congress of Nations is a congress of ambassadors, who may be empowered to make these treaty stipulations. Burlamaqui, however, is of opinion, that all felons should be given up, without any treaty stipulations. With respect to persons, charged with political crimes in time of civil war and commotion, and refugees from conquered countries, the case is more difficult. Nations may agree to warn such characters away, especially if demanded by the nation from whence they come, and more especially if they should be reasonably suspected of forming plots and conspiracies against their own country; but it would be hard to give them up, if innocent of any such thing, at least until the excitement in their own country had subsided.

4. A Congress of Nations is the only place where measures may be concerted, effectually to suppress the slave trade and piracy. Nations, when represented in a general congress, would more willingly give up the slave trade; and more willingly allow their vessels to be searched for slaves. Measures could be agreed on, which would nearly put a stop to piracy; but if wars cease, piracy will cease of course, for war is the nursery of pirates.

* 39   * 5. Some mutual understanding and cooperation in making railroads and canals across the isthmus of Darien and Suez, might be agreed on, and the erection of lights and buoys on uninhabited or barbarous coasts and straits much frequented by civilized nations might be attempted by this Congress, and the principles of salvage on

wrecked property and vessels abandoned at sea might be better defined.

6. The subjects of international patents and copy-rights might be attended to by this Congress, and some progress might be made toward an international post-office, to extend all over the world. Neither is it too much to expect, that the time may come, when an universal standard of weights, measures and coins will be settled by such a Congress.

7. The general principle of the free navigation of bays and rivers might be established by this Congress, and thus many inconveniences and, perhaps, wars saved. It seems perfectly reasonable, that a nation possessing one bank of a navigable river, but whose territory does not extend quite to the ocean, should have a right to the free navigation of that river, especially if she possesses both of the banks, but not the mouth. It is true, much may be said for and against this principle, and a Congress of Nations is the place in which to say it.

8. The right of discovery and colonization has never yet been settled. A want of a proper understanding of this subject has been the cause of many wars.

9. In a Congress of Nations, measures could be agreed upon for the reduction of the vast military * 40 and * naval establishments of Christendom, which are such an intolerable burden on the community, consuming seven-eighths of the income of nations. One nation keeps up these immense establishments because another does. If nations would agree to reduce their establishments, it could be done with safety and advantage. If the number of ships could not be restrained, the size might be, and no nation be allowed to have a ship of war above a certain size, or to carry more than a certain weight of metal.

10. This Congress would be the proper place to agree on the general restoration of all military trophies and captured standards. The retention of these trophies, and the vain-glorious display of them in temples dedicated to the Prince of peace, is no less an insult to common sense, than it is an impious desecration of these solemn temples. It is a relic of heathenism, which ought, long ago, to have been abandoned by all nations bearing the Christian name. To restore these trophies to the nations from which they were captured, would be no less wise than magnanimous. But it would be best of all, if some place were selected, near the location of the Congress of Nations, where all the captured standards and other trophies of war, — except works of art, which should be restored to their former owners, — should be piled together in one vast heap, and consumed. It would be a burnt-offering worthy of the cause of peace. The metallic parts, having passed the ordeal of the fire, might be coined into medallions, with suitable devices and inscriptions, and circulated through the world.

Something of this kind was done at Madrid, July * 41　1, 1823. * " Agreeably to arrangements made, fifty non-commissioned officers and veterans of the French army, each carrying one of the Spanish standards, which, during the late wars, had been taken by the French, repaired to the palace of the Regency, and restored those trophies to the Saloons of the Columns. The ceremony was conducted with great pomp." * For the same reasons, the names of bridges, palaces, &c., which have been named from some great victory, should be changed; and triumphal arches and other monuments of war should be demolished, and the materials taken to erect hospitals, colleges, and churches. This appears to the present age Utopian; but it is no more

* Boston Sentinel, of Sept. 8, 1823.

Utopian than a millennium, when men will beat their swords into ploughshares and their spears into pruning-hooks. Centuries may roll away before this grand consummation, so devoutly to be wished, will take place, but it will be done.

11. There are many other subjects, of a pacific and civil nature, which might be discussed in a Congress of Nations, and settled, if advisable, or put into a train of settlement. These may come up, from time to time, as the world advances in Christianity and civilization. The Congress might continue to sit, for the settlement of these questions, so far as practicable; but at any time of its session, it might take up the great subject of a COURT OF NATIONS, and take measures for its organization. This is the subject of the next chapter.

*CHAPTER VII.

A COURT OF NATIONS FOR THE PEACEFUL ADJUDICATION OF THOSE CASES OF INTERNATIONAL DIFFICULTY WHICH SHOULD BE REFERRED TO IT, BY THE MUTUAL CONSENT OF TWO OR MORE NATIONS.

1. Organization—2. Appointment of members—3. A majority to decide disputes—4. Rules of the Court—5. Cases of disputed boundary—6. To act as a mediator—7. May judge cases of right of succession, if called on by both parties—8. Suggest laws to the Congress—9. Other things to be done by them.

1. IT is proposed to organize a Court of Nations, composed of as many members as the Congress of Nations shall previously agree upon, say two from each of the powers represented at the Congress. The power of the court to be merely advisory. It is to act as a high court of admiralty, but without its enforcing powers. There is to be no sheriff, or posse, to enforce its commands. It is to take cognizance only of such cases as shall be referred to it, by the free and mutual consent of both parties concerned, like a chamber of commerce; and is to have no more power to enforce its decisions than an ecclesiastical court in this country.

2. The members of this court are to be appointed by the governments represented in the Congress *43 of * Nations, and shall hold their places according to the tenure previously agreed on in the Congress — probably during good behaviour. Whether they should be paid by the governments sending them, or by the nations represented in the Congress conjointly, according to the ratio of their population or wealth, may be agreed on in the Congress. The court should organize itself by choosing

a president and vice-presidents from among themselves, and appoint the necessary clerks, secretaries, reporters, &c.; and they should hear counsel on both sides of the questions to be judged. They might meet once a year for the transaction of business, and adjourn to such time and place as they should think proper. Their meeting should never be in a country which had a case on trial. These persons should enjoy the same privileges and immunities as ambassadors.

3. Their verdicts, like the verdicts of other great courts, should be decided by a majority, and need not be, like the decrees of the Congress, unanimous. The majority should appoint one of their number to make out their verdict, giving a statement of facts from the testimony presented to the court, and the reasoning on those facts by which they come to a conclusion.

4. All cases submitted to the court should be judged by the true interpretation of existing treaties, and by the laws enacted by the Congress and ratified by the nations represented; and where these treaties and laws fail
* 44 of establishing the point at issue, they * should judge the cause by the principles of equity and justice.

5. In cases of disputed boundary, the court should have the power to send surveyors appointed by themselves, but at the expense of the parties, to survey the boundaries, collect facts on the spot, and report to the court. Had there been such a court, the boundary line between Maine and New Brunswick would, long ago, have been equitably settled, to the satisfaction of both parties. Some of the ex-governors of Maine have expressed to me that opinion. The Supreme Court of the United States, very soon, settled a similar difficulty between Massachusetts and Rhode Island.

6. This court should not only decide on all cases brought before it by any two or more independent, contending nations, but they should be authorized to offer their mediation where war actually exists, or in any difficulty arising between any two or more nations which would endanger the peace of the world. Indeed, they should act as conservators of the peace of Christendom, and watch over the welfare of mankind, either of the nations of the confederacy, or the world at large. Often nations go to war on a point of honor; and having begun to threaten, think they cannot recede without disgrace; at the same time, they would be glad to catch at such an excuse for moderation; and often, when nations are nearly exhausted by a protracted war, they would be glad to make peace, but they fear to make the first advances, lest it should be imputed to weakness; * 45 and * they would joyfully embrace a mediator. In cases where ambassadors would neither be sent nor accepted, the members of this court might go, as heralds of peace. How much better it would have been for the honor and interest of France, if she had submitted her late disputes with Mexico, Buenos Ayres and queen Pomare, to such a court, rather than be at so great an expense to force an unwilling confession, which will rankle in the hearts of those who have been forced to it, for a whole generation.

7. If the court should be applied to, to settle any internal dispute between any two contending factions, such as the right of succession to the throne, it would be their duty to hear the parties, and give their opinion according to the laws and usages of the country asking their advice; but they should never officiously offer an exparte verdict, though they might propose terms of reconciliation. It is probable, that, had such a court existed, the troubles in Spain and Portugal would have been of short duration.

8. It should be the duty of a Court of Nations, from time to time, to suggest topics for the consideration of the Congress, as new or unsettled principles, favorable to the peace and welfare of nations, would present themselves to the court, in the adjudication of cases. They would be the more able to do this, from their being more than all other men conversant with such subjects, and their intimations would be well received by the Congress, who should in all their acts, study the good of mankind and * 46   the * interests of humanity; so that in doubtful cases philanthropy should be thrown into the scale.

9. There are many other cases beside those above-mentioned, in which such a court would either prevent war or end it. A nation would not be justified, in the opinion of the world, in going to war, when there was an able and impartial umpire to judge its case; and many a dispute would be quashed at the outset, if it were known that the world would require an impartial investigation of it by able judges.

*CHAPTER VIII.

HISTORICAL NOTICES OF PAST ATTEMPTS AT SOMETHING LIKE A CONGRESS AND COURT OF NATIONS.

1. Plans in some things resembling this very ancient—2. Amphictyonic Council— 3. Achæan League—4. Lycian Confederacy—5. League of the Hanse towns— 7. Great scheme of Henry IV—8. Holy Alliance—9-22. Congress of Panama —23. Inferences to be deduced from it—24. Remarks on the foregoing— 25. Some of their features retained—26. Number of delegates.

1. FROM the history of the earliest ages, it appears that mankind have been desirous of something like the proposed plan of a Congress and Court of Nations, especially in communities of small independent states, where from the contiguity of the parties, such a plan was more easy to be carried into effect, and was more necessary for their safety and happiness. In most of these confederations, protection from external violence was as much an object as internal peace. There were, therefore, many features in ancient councils, diets, and congresses, which do not at all enter into *our* plan, and which sooner or later paved the way for the ruin of *theirs*. Nevertheless, while they did continue, they were a great blessing to the parties concerned. We, by no means, propose them as models for our plan, but adduce them, only to show that, if so great an advance

  towards the perfection of civil society could be made
* 48   in times of * ignorance, superstition and barbarity,
  much more is to be expected from a somewhat similar
plan, in this age of reason, philanthropy, and Christianity. After reviewing these plans, I shall attempt to show wherein

they differed from that which we propose, and also what parts of them are to be retained in our plan, and what rejected from it.

2. The Council of the Amphictyons consisted originally of twelve states or cities, and finally extended to thirty-one. It was established in the year 1497, B. C. Rollin says, " It was, in a manner, the holding of a general assembly of the states of Greece. Its establishment is attributed to Amphictyon, king of Athens, who gave it his name. His principal view was to unite, in the sacred bond of amity, the several states of Greece admitted into it, and oblige them, by that union, to undertake the defence of each other, and *be mutually vigilant for the happiness and tranquillity of their country.* It was held at Thermopylæ and sometimes at Delphos, and regularly assembled in the spring and fall, and oftener if occasion required. Each city sent two deputies, and consequently had two votes in the council, and that without distinction, or the more powerful having any prerogative of honor or preeminence over inferior states in regard to the suffrages — the liberty, on which these people valued themselves, requiring that every thing should be equal among them. *They had full power to discuss all differences which might arise between the Amphictyonic cities."* Rees, in his Cyclopædia says, *" They decided all public differences and disputes between any of* * 49 *the * cities of Greece,* and their determinations were received with the greatest veneration, and were ever held sacred and inviolable. Had its members been actuated by a spirit of peace, of justice and of good order, it would have rendered it for ever respectable." But Philip, king of Macedon, by his intrigues, gained an ascendency in this famous council, and was the means of reducing it to a mere shadow. Nevertheless it continued until after the reign of

Augustus Cæsar, or for fifteen centuries, and gradually expired.

3. Of the Achæan League, Rees says, " Strangers to the desire of conquest, and having little connection with corrupt nations, they never employed falsehood, even against their enemies. Although each city was independent of the others, yet they formed one body and one state. So great was their character for justice and probity, that the Greek cities of Italy referred their disputes to their arbitration. The Lacedemonians and Thebans referred to them an interesting matter of dissension between them. Having long retained their liberty, they ceased not to assemble when the necessity of public deliberation required it, and even when the rest of Greece was threatened with war and pestilence." Polybius observes, " The Achæans so far gained the esteem and confidence of all the Europeans, that their name became common to all that country." The Achæan League, however, at length fell into discord, and became, in consequence, like the Amphictyons, subject to the Lacedemonians. But 280 years before Christ the league was renewed, and continued 134 years longer.

* 50   * 4. The Lycian Confederacy consisted of twenty-three cities, in which a monarchical form of government prevailed. In the general council, the large cities had three votes, the smaller two. They had once been addicted to piracy; but Rees says, " The Lycians are highly commended by the ancients for their sobriety and manner of administering justice."

5. The league of the Hanse towns commenced in the 12th century, and was confirmed and established in the year 1234. An extraordinary general assembly was held every ten years, in which they solemnly renewed their league, admitted new members and expelled old ones, if they proved refractory.

This confederation first commenced by a league between the cities of Lubeck and Hamburgh, and afterward consisted of twelve towns situated near the Baltic. They first formed a *system of international laws, enacted in their general assemblies.* The league afterward extended to between seventy and eighty towns and cities. In the year 1730, the regular number was sixty-three, besides which there were forty-four towns that were considered as allies. While they kept at peace with the surrounding nations, they flourished beyond all precedent, but having become rich and powerful, they equipped fleets and raised armies; and about the year 1346, they waged a successful war against Waldemar III, king of Denmark; and again against the same power in 1428. By this means, they drew on them the jealousy of other powers, and the league was gradually reduced; so that

the present Hanseatic League consists only of the
* 51   three cities, Lubeck, * Hamburgh, and Bremen;

and in the definitive treaty of 1803, they were acknowledged as Hanseatic cities, with a guaranty of their jurisprudence and perpetual neutrality.

6. The foundation of the confederation of the states of Switzerland, commonly called the Helvetic Union, was laid in 1308. Rees says, " The code of public law between the combined republics of Switzerland is founded on the treaty of Sempatch in 1393, upon the convention of Stantz, and the treaty of peace in 1712, at Arau, between the Protestant and Catholic cantons. From these several treaties it appears, that the Helvetic Union is a perpetual defensive alliance between independent powers, to protect each other by their united force against all foreign enemies. Another essential object of the league is, to *preserve general peace and good order;* for which purpose it is covenanted, that *all public dissensions shall finally be settled between the con-*

*tending parties in an amicable manner; and with this view
particular judges and arbitrators are appointed, who shall
be empowered to compose the dissensions which may happen
to arise.* To this is added a reciprocal guaranty of the forms
of government established in the respective commonwealths.
No separate engagement, which any of the cantons may
conclude, can be valid if it be inconsistent with the fundamental articles of this general union. With these exceptions,
the combined states are independent of each other. They
may form alliances with any power, or may reject the same,
though all the others have acceded to it — may grant
* 52 auxiliary troops * to foreign princes — may prohibit
the money of the other cantons from being current
within their own territories — may impose taxes, and, in
short, perform every other act of absolute sovereignty. The
public affairs of the Helvetic body are discussed and determined in their several diets." " The ordinary meeting of
the *general* diet is in January, annually, and continues
sitting one month. The extraordinary assemblies are
summoned upon particular occasions." " Each canton
sends as many deputies as it thinks proper." " The whole
republic is composed of thirteen cantons, thirteen incorporated territories and twenty-one independent lordships."
" Every town and state has its own particular constitution
for the management of its churches, academies, schools and
other ecclesiastical affairs; but *all live in mutual amity,
without invading the rights and privileges of one another.*"
J. Mallet Du Pan, who seems to have been an inhabitant of
Switzerland, and probably a native, in his " History of the
Destruction of the Helvetic Union," published in London,
in 1798, says of the Helvetic Confederacy, " Those states,
united for their common preservation, consisted of twenty
republics, forming one republic, and, notwithstanding the

defect of a collective body without sovereignty, experience promised it duration; for *the imperfection of its federal union was counterbalanced by great advantages.* If it enfeebled subordination in those aggregate communities, it also left them with independence, the invaluable privilege of obeying their own laws and of being governed by * 53 their immediate fellow-citizens." * " The relations and duties of this defensive league were settled by simple agreement, and their sanction was ratified by time and self-interest. No treacherous idea of an *independent* republic ever entered the minds of these sensible people. Nature and fortune had made them unequal in territory, in political liberty, manners, and origin; they respected nature and the work of ages." A writer in the Christian Spectator of 1832, says, " No diversities of character and state are greater than those which exist in this confederation. It comprises people of three distinct nations, speaking three of the prominent languages of Europe, — the German in the east, the French in the west, and the Italian in the south-east. They are divided into twenty-two independent states, each of which has a dress and manners, in some degree, peculiar to itself, and a dialect often scarcely intelligent to those around it. The forms of government vary, from the purest democracy, in which every male of the canton above the age of seventeen is a member of the body which makes the laws, to the most rigorous aristocracy, in which the offices are confined almost entirely to the families of patricians. The nature of the confederation is not such as to impress a uniform character on elements so discordant. Their *diet is a mere convention of ambassadors, who only treat with each other according to the strict tenor of their instructions,* and who cannot vote for a law without first obtaining the consent of the government which sends them."

It is difficult, but not important, to reconcile the dis-
crepancies of these * writers, with respect to the number of the members of this Union. Perhaps the
number has been different at different times. Some members may have been excluded, or withdrawn, and others
added. All these writers agree, however, in the main
features of the Union; and show that it consisted of numbers
of *independent* states, differing from one another in language, religion, laws, forms of government, manners and
customs, united together, not only for the purpose of resisting foreign aggression, but for the purpose of maintaining
peace with one another, by an equitable and amicable
settlement of all disputes arising between any two or more
members of the Union, which has continued for more than
500 years to be a blessing to the framers of it and their
posterity. It is true the whirlwind of the French revolution,
which prostrated every thing else within its vortex, nearly
upset this gallant bark also, so that many, with J. Mallet
Du Pan, thought her destroyed. But the storm passed over,
and she righted again, by the weight of her own ballast,
and she now keeps on the peaceful tenor of her way, the
admiration of the world and a beautiful monument of human
wisdom. I have dwelt the longer on the Helvetic Union,
because I consider the civil part of this institution — the diet
and the court of judges or arbitrators — as the nearest
working model of our proposed Congress and Court of
Nations which ever existed. True, it is imperfect, like all
other human devices, and wants that correction, which the
increased knowledge and wisdom of the present
times can give it. * No good reason can be given
why a plan, which has worked so well on a small
scale, may not be extended, so as to embrace all Christian
and civilized nations.

* 54

* 55

7. The Great Scheme of Henry IV, of France, begun in 1601, here requires a passing notice. The real object of Henry is uncertain, — possibly it was defence against the encroachments of Mahometan nations on Christendom, — probably the humbling of the house of Austria. Whatever were his motives, he imagined the great project of uniting all the nations of Europe in one grand confederated republic of fifteen members — six hereditary monarchies, five elective monarchies, and four republics. He gained the consent of Holland, Hesse Cassel, Anhalt, Hungary, Bohemia, Lower Austria, several provinces and towns in Germany, the Swiss cantons, and queen Elizabeth of England. The limits of this dissertation do not allow me to go further into the details of a plan, which, in the moral state of the world when it was proposed, never could have been accomplished; and if it had been, the condition of mankind, probably, would not have been immediately much ameliorated; for they might have lost as much in liberty as they would have gained in a peace compelled by the power of the sword and great standing armies, always dangerous to liberty and the favorite instrument of tyrants. The assassin Ravaillac put an end, at once, to the Great Scheme and the life of the great Henry, in 1610, and nothing remains of the Scheme, but its record in history. All that the friends of peace would make of the Great Scheme is, to show that, if so * 56   many * nations could be induced to embrace a plan so complicated, cumbersome, and expensive, we have abundant reason to believe, that a plan so simple, easy, and cheap as that which we propose, would at once be adopted by Christian nations, if once proposed by some leading power.

8. The Holy Alliance is the next thing of the kind which claims our attention. An extraordinary instrument, of three short articles, dated at Paris, September, 1815, was signed

and sealed by Francis, emperor of Austria, Frederic William, king of Prussia, and Alexander, emperor of Russia. The three articles barely state, for substance, that the high contracting parties solemnly pledge themselves to behave like brethren in their future intercourse with one another, to assist each other, and to be fathers to their subjects. They acknowledge God as the only rightful sovereign, and that the world "has in reality no other sovereign than Him." They commend the principles of the Christian religion to their subjects; and they offer to receive other nations professing like principles into their alliance. The emperor Alexander issued a manifesto, on the Christmas following, in which he ordered the articles of the Alliance to be read in all the churches in Russia. In that manifesto, he promised to adopt " the principle derived from the words and religion of our Lord and Saviour Jesus Christ, who teaches mankind to live as brethren, not in hatred and strife, but in peace and love." It does not appear, that any other of the nations, except the abovementioned, have joined the Holy *57   Alliance, though the kings of * England and France sent ministers to them, not, however, as sovereigns, but as individuals. It was said, that there was a constitutional objection to Great Britain's joining the Alliance, as mentioned in the succeeding note. It has been looked on with jealousy by the free people of other countries, as a conspiracy of kings against the liberty of their subjects; but I have no doubt that Alexander, who was the father and chief promoter of the enterprise, meant better things. His premature death, together with this jealousy, was probably the cause why the Holy Alliance came to nothing.*   From

* The following extract of a letter from ex-president Adams to the author, shows his opinion of the Holy Alliance:

"The Holy Alliance itself was a tribute from the mightiest men of the

what has appeared in some English periodicals, it is probable, that the plan of the Holy Alliance was first suggested to Alexander, when he was in London, by an English lady.

    9. The Congress of Panama is the last thing *58 of * the kind of which I propose to give an account, and, as it is an event of great importance to us, as an attempt at something more like the very plan which has always been the object of the friends of peace than any of the preceding; and as it is but little known or understood, either in America or Europe, I shall depart from the plan hitherto pursued in this chapter, of devoting but one section to each of the past attempts at an approximation to a Congress of Nations. I spent a part of last winter (1838–9) at Washington, principally in order to collect facts and documents on this and other subjects interesting to the cause of peace. All the documents of the House of Representatives were politely laid open to me, and I was much assisted by the urbanity and intelligence of the gentleman who has the charge of them. The following extracts were made from those documents.

10. President Adams, in his message to both Houses of Congress, dated December 6, 1825, thus notices the Congress

European world to the purity of your principles and the practicability of your system for the general preservation of peace. The poisonous ingredient in that league was the *unlimited* sovereignty of the parties to it. The league was *autocratic*, and so peculiar was this feature in its composition, that the prince regent of Great Britain, when invited to become a party to it, because the constitution of that country did not recognize treaties as national, under the personal signature of the monarch, [declined.] The professed principles of the Holy Alliance were the perpetual preservation of peace, and the sovereigns who signed the treaty, declared that they considered the Christian principles of benevolence, mutual forbearance and charity, as obligatory upon them as *scvereigns* equally as upon individuals. But they bound themselves to support each other against all wrong-doers (they themselves to be the judges of the wrong), not only of foreigners, but of their own subjects."

of Panama and the South American states: "Among the measures which have been suggested to them, by the new relations to one another, resulting from the recent changes in their condition, is that of assembling, at the isthmus of Panama, a congress, at which each of them shall be represented, to deliberate on objects important to the welfare of them all. The republics of Colombia, of Mexico, and of Central America have already deputed plenipotentiaries to such a meeting, and they have invited the United States to be also represented there by their ministers. The * 59 invitation has been accepted, * and ministers on the part of the United States will be commissioned to attend at those deliberations, and to take part in them, so far as can be compatible with that neutrality, from which it is neither the intention, nor the desire, of the other American states that we should depart."

11. On March 7, 1826, President Adams sent a special message to the House of Representatives, in answer to their requirement, from which the following facts and observations are obtained. It appears that before instructions had been given to our ministers to Panama, treaties had been entered into by the republics of South America. In this message, Mr. Adams observes, " In the intercourse between nations, temper is a minister, perhaps more powerful than talent. Nothing was ever lost by kind treatment. Nothing can be gained by sullen repulses and aspiring pretensions." " Objects of the highest importance, not only to the future welfare of the whole human race, but bearing directly on the special interests of this Union, will engage the deliberations of the Congress of Panama, whether we are represented there or not. Others, if we are represented, may be offered by our plenipotentiaries for consideration, having in view both these great results — our own interests and the improve-

ment of the condition of man upon earth. It may be that, in the lapse of many centuries, no other opportunity so favorable will be presented to the government of the United States, to subserve the benevolent purposes of Divine Providence, to dispense the promised blessings of the * 60 Redeemer of mankind, * to promote the prevalence, in future ages, of peace on earth and good-will to man, as will now be placed in their power by participating in the deliberations of this congress."

12. The President further adds, " It will be in the recollection of the House that, immediately after the war of our independence, a measure, closely analogous to this Congress of Panama, was adopted by the Congress of our confederation, and for purposes of precisely the same character. Three commissioners, with plenipotentiary powers, were appointed, to negotiate treaties of amity, navigation, and commerce with all the principal powers of Europe. They met and resided about one year, for that purpose, at Paris; and the result of their negotiations, at that time, was the first treaty between the United States and Prussia — remarkable in the diplomatic annals of the world, and precious as a monument of the principles in relation to commerce and maritime warfare, with which our country entered into her career as a member of the great family of independent nations. This treaty, prepared in conformity with the instructions of the American plenipotentiaries, consecrated three fundamental principles of foreign intercourse, which the Congress of that period were desirous of establishing. First, equal reciprocity and the mutual stipulation of the privileges of the most favored nation in the commercial exchanges of peace; secondly, *the abolition of private war on the ocean;* and, thirdly, *restrictions favorable to neutral commerce upon belligerent practices with regard*

to contraband of war and blockades."   " They
* 61   were * able to obtain from one great and philosophical, though absolute, sovereign of Europe
[Frederick III, of Prussia] an assent to their liberal and
enlightened principles."

13. Speaking of the republics of South America, the
President adds, " The only causes of dissension between us
and them which ever have arisen, originated in those never-
failing fountains of discord and irritation, discriminations
of commercial favor to other countries, *licentious privateers,
and paper blockades."* He further adds, " If it be true,
that the noblest treaty of peace ever mentioned in history,
is that by which the Carthaginians were bound to abolish the
practice of sacrificing their own children *because it was
stipulated in favor of human nature,* I cannot exaggerate
to myself the unfading glory, with which these United States
will go forth in the memory of future ages, if by their friendly
counsel, by their moral influence, by the power of argument
and persuasion alone, they can prevail upon the American
nations at Panama to stipulate by general agreement among
themselves, and so far as any of them may be concerned,
the perpetual abolition of private war upon the ocean.   And
if we cannot yet flatter ourselves, that this can be accomplished, as advances toward it, the establishment of the
principle, that *the friendly flag shall cover the cargo, the
curtailment of the contraband of war, and the proscription
of fictitious paper blockades;* engagements, which we may
reasonably hope will not prove impracticable, will, if successfully inculcated, redound proportionably to our honor,
* 62   and drain the fountain * of many a future, sanguinary
war."   The President closed his message with the
following remarks: " That the Congress of Panama will
accomplish all, or even any of the transcendent benefits to

the human race which warmed the conception of its first purpose, it is perhaps indulging too sanguine a forecast of events to promise. It is in its nature speculative and experimental. The blessings of heaven may turn it to the account of human improvement. Accidents unforeseen and mischances not to be anticipated may baffle all its high purposes and disappoint its fairest expectations. But the design is great. It looks to the amelioration of the condition of man."

14. Accompanying this message was a communication from Henry Clay, Secretary of State, giving an account of the first intimation, which was made to him, of the proposed Congress of Panama, which intimation was made during the preceding spring, in a conversation with the ministers of Colombia and Mexico on the same day. Don Jose Maria Salazar, minister from Colombia, wrote a letter to Mr. Clay, under date of November 2, 1825, in which he reminds him of a previous conversation on the subject of the proposed Congress, and Mr. Clay's intimation that, if the United States were formally invited, they would send a delegate to it. This letter is intended to be the formal invitation, at the same time informing Mr. Clay that the " minister from Mexico will present the same on the part of his government; and that the minister from Guatemala has just received similar instructions from his government." Don * 63 Pablo Obregen, the minister from * Mexico, afterwards extended a similar formal invitation, in which he states, that the Congress was to assemble at Panama, and that " representatives from Colombia, Peru, Guatemala, and Mexico will have arrived at the date of this letter," (Nov. 3, 1825.) Don Antonio Jose Cañar, minister from the government of Central America, in a letter to Mr. Clay, of near the same date, joins in the invitation, and states, that

his government had formed a convention with Colombia on the 19th of March preceding, providing for this object.

15. On the abovementioned message of the President, it seems Mr. Crowninshield, of the committee of Foreign Affairs, offered a report, dated March 26, 1826, of which the following are some of the features. 1st. The report replies to the objection that the proposed Congress is unconstitutional, and plainly shows its constitutionality. 2d. It replies to the objection, " that all its objects could be attained by separate negotiation with the several states," and thus answers that objection. " It is questionable whether separate and disconnected negotiations between states, geographically so remote and in various respects politically different from each other, *could* be brought to the same harmonious and systematic result as a discussion in an assembly of diplomatic agents, promptly communicating with each other information, counsel, and argument." Another objection answered is, that of an " entangling alliance." It was shown, that there is no more danger in an alliance with all the

* 64 nations together, than in an * alliance with each separately, especially when it is understood, that no act of our ministers at the Congress would be binding, until ratified by our government. Another objection answered in the report is, that the proposed Congress is unprecedented. But there have been many congresses of a like nature in Europe, and if this objection ever had any force, it is now void. The adoption of the federal constitution of the United States was equally unprecedented.

16. It would be very interesting, to insert the whole of this very able report. Almost all the arguments, used to support the policy of sending representatives to the Congress of Panama, would apply to the case of a Congress of Nations; while some objections which appeared specious,

when urged against the Congress of Panama, are of no force when urged against a general Congress of Nations. While this report was under consideration in the House, several resolutions, hostile to it, were introduced, but their aim seemed to be chiefly directed against any *political* connection; but to a representative in a *diplomatic* character, there seemed to be no forcible objection.

17. Brevity compels me barely to notice a few facts and dates of importance, like the following. The emperor of Brazil appointed a plenipotentiary to attend the Congress of Panama, by a decree dated January 25, 1826. On March 26, 1826, President Adams submitted to the consideration of Congress the propriety of making the appropriation necessary to carry into effect the Congress of Panama.

The commissions of the ministers from the United * 65   States * to the Congress of Panama, are dated March 14, 1826. Mr. Anderson, one of our ministers left Bogota, to repair to Panama, June 12, 1826. Mr. Sargeant, our other minister, commenced his legation on the 24th of October of the same year. The Congress of Panama was organized 22d of June, 1826. The session was a short one, on account of the sickliness of the climate of Panama, most of the delegates being affected with it; and it was adjourned to meet at Tacubaya, near the city of Mexico, July 15th, of the following year. An agent was sent by the governments of Great Britain, of France, and of the Netherlands, but it does not appear that either arrived in time to be present at the first congress. Neither of the envoys from the United States arrived in time for the first session. The only members represented were Peru, Mexico, Central America, and Colombia. Plenipotentiaries were expected from Chili, but there was not time for their appointment and arrival.

18. One of the subjects to be discussed at Panama was,

the right of a civilized nation so to occupy uncivilized countries, by colonies, as to exclude others. One object of our sending commissioners to Panama was to secure to our citizens their religious rights in the various countries of South America. A similar subject might, perhaps, engage the attention of a Congress of Nations. The Colombian minister at Washington, in one of his communications to our government, says, " At Panama, the best and most opportune occasion is offered to the United States, to *fix some* principles *of international law, the unsettled* * *state of which has done much evil to humanity."* Another thing proposed by him was a treaty offensive and defensive against the aggressions of Spain. This, after all, perhaps was the chief object of the South American republics for calling the Congress; but this, of course, the United States would have nothing to do with, having always adopted a neutral policy. The rights of neutrals, the suppression of the African slave trade, and the independence of Hayti, were among the other objects proposed, perhaps for a lure, to our government.

19. As no delegates had arrived from any foreign nation, in time to take part in the deliberations of the first session of the Congress, none of those things of general interest to the civilized world at large were agitated, but they only busied themselves with South American concerns, perhaps from a conviction, that it would be useless to discuss topics of general interest, in so small a Congress. The business done was, " 1st. A treaty of union, league, and perpetual confederation, between the four American states represented at the Congress, to which the other powers of America might accede within a year. 2d. A convention for the renewal of the great assembly annually in time of war, and tri-annually in time of peace. 3d. A convention which fixes the contingent

which each confederate should contribute for the common defence. 4th. An arrangement concerning the employment and direction of those contingents. 5th. Divers declarations, that the treaties which Colombia had formerly con-
* 67   cluded with the United * Mexican States, Central America, and Peru, should be included in those treaties with certain reservations."

20. This is all that was done at the Congress of Panama, and probably none of it would have been done in that Congress, had the delegates appointed by the other powers arrived in time to take a part in the discussions. But these delegates from the South American states, finding themselves alone, did not venture on the discussion of those topics which were proposed by those states when they invited other powers to join them in a Congress of Nations; and they acted only on those which were peculiarly interesting to themselves, and which would not have been thought proper subjects of discussion in a congress of delegates from the principal powers of Christendom. What were some of the principal objects aimed at by the Congress of Panama may be learned from the introductory or, probably, inaugural speech of the minister from Peru — for which see Appendix, No. 1.

21. In a conversation which I held with Mr. Sargeant, at Washington, January 29, 1839, I learned, that he went to Tacubaya, at the time appointed, and found there but two or three delegates, — whether Mr. Anderson was one of them I do not know, or whether he attended *any* meeting of the Congress, — but no congress was organized at Tacubaya, and there the thing ended. I did not find Mr. Sargeant very communicative — perhaps on account of ill health and
* 68   a pressing engagement on his hands, which * required his immediate attention. I had no opportunity to

call on him afterward. Diligent search was made, among the congressional documents, for a report from the delegation to Panama, but it was not found. I have since written to Mr. Sargeant for a copy of such a report, but have received no answer. Probably such a report was never made.

22. The causes of the failure of the Congress of Panama, and the reasons why it did not become a Congress of Nations, deserve a passing notice. 1st. The South Americans were not *the people* to commence such a congress — just emerged as they were from a state of semi-barbarism and slavery, they knew little, or nothing, of the principles of international law — and, besides this, they were more intent on securing their own independence from Spain, than establishing a system of pacific relations with all other nations. They were, themselves, at war at the time, and could attend to nothing but war. The government, that invites a Congress of Nations, must be in perfect peace and harmony with all other governments. 2d. Panama was not the *place* for such a congress, far removed as it was from intercourse with the rest of the world, and very sickly. Could the Congress have been held together until our ambassadors and the delegates from other enlightened states could have met with them, something might, nevertheless, have been done; but, interrupted by an endemical sickness, they scattered, never again to be united. Had President Adams, when invited to attend to this subject, only requested, that the proposed congress should be
* 69   held * at Washington or Philadelphia, the South American ministers could not have objected, many more delegates would have been sent by the powers of Europe, a Congress of Nations would have commenced, and a new and happy era would have dawned on the world. 3d. The *character of Bolivar,* under whose auspices the congress was called, was another obstacle to its success. More intent

on extending his own power than on preserving peace, he found that the congress would be an obstacle to his ambitious designs, and he therefore withdrew his countenance from it. I am confirmed in this opinion, by a letter from ex-president Adams to me, dated September 14, 1838, of which the following is an extract: " The proposition [for a congress of the South American nations] originated, I believe, with the late Doctor William Thornton, of Washington; who addressed a memoir, recommending a congress of the American republics, to a distinguished citizen of Venezuela, through whom it was communicated to Bolivar, the Napoleon of this hemisphere. Bolivar had no more honest regard for peace or human liberty than had his prototype in Europe, but he had liberated, conquered, and constituted the republic of Colombia — he was pursuing his conquests into Peru, and constituting another mock republic there, and was wearing himself out in projects of investing his brow with an imperial crown, sparkling before his eyes, like the dagger before the vision of Macbeth. Bolivar thought that a Congress of Nations at Panama might serve to promote some of

* 70   his own ambitious purposes, * and he made the proposition. The other emancipated colonies, how-ever, and especially the Mexicans, were jealous of his designs, and had counter projects of their own."

23. The inference to be deduced from this abortive attempt at a Congress of Nations is, that the governments of Christendom are willing to send delegates to any such Congress, whenever it shall be called *by a respectable state,* well established in its own government, if called in a time of peace, to meet at a proper place. That this attempt at a Congress of Nations, or even a dozen more, should prove abortive on account of defects in their machinery or materials, ought not to discourage us, any more than the dozen incipient

attempts at a steam-boat, which proved abortive for similar reasons, should have discouraged Fulton. Every failure throws new light on this subject, which is founded in the principles of truth and equity. Some monarch, president, or statesman — some moral Fulton, as great in ethics as he was in physics, will yet arise, and complete this great moral machine, so as to make it practically useful, but improvable by coming generations. Before the fame of such a man, your Cæsars, Alexanders, and Napoleons will hide their diminished heads, as the twinkling stars of night fade away before the glory of the full-orbed king of day. It is remarkable that the first intimation of the last two abortive attempts at a Congress of Nations, — abortive because deficient in constitution and materials, — should have been suggested by a private individual.

* 71   * 24. My *remarks on the past attempts at something like a Congress and Court of Nations,* mentioned in this chapter, must be few. It is obvious to the reader of history, that I have selected but few out of the great number of these attempts, both in ancient and modern times; but I have taken those with which the general reader is best acquainted, except the congress of Panama, which is comparatively recent and unknown, and in which our country was much interested; and, therefore, it required a more extended development. It is equally obvious, that from the earliest ages, mankind have been desirous of something like the proposed Congress and Court of Nations, especially in communities of small independent states, when, from the contiguity of the parties, such a plan was the more easy to be carried into effect, and more necessary to their safety, peace and happiness. Many of these attempts were eminently successful; and though they partook of the instability of all sublunary things; while they did continue, they were a great blessing to the parties concerned, and often to surrounding nations.

25. There are some features in these past attempts, which would be retained by us, as essential to our plan; and some as decidedly rejected. We should adopt the pacific part of their plans, which was to secure peace and equity among themselves, though it was but a secondary consideration to them, as necessary to their existence as a confederation. With us, this pacific principle is the chief motive. The other has no weight at all. Ought we not to suppose, *72 that * in this enlightened age of the world, this chief motive would be sufficient to induce Christian nations to make the safe and cheap attempt, when the good to be obtained by success is commensurate only with the extent and duration of the world? Is it too much to hope that, in this age of reason and philanthropy, the preservation of peace, equity, and justice, and the avoidance of all the sins and horrors of war may be a sufficient motive to induce Christian nations to try the experiment recommended in these Essays? Our plan would not essentially change the existing relations of nations towards each other with respect to peace and war, by any *direct* influence on the subject. It is only a general treaty entered into, by all the nations with each, and by each nation with all, that henceforth they will endeavor to settle their controversies with one another by the law of reason, as becomes rational creatures, and not by the law of violence which becomes only brutes; and that if war be necessary in the nature of things, and men will fight, they shall mutually, and jointly, and severally agree, that they will abandon some of the most barbarous features of war, and protect the peaceful; and that they will seek those things which make for the peace and happiness of mankind at large. Therefore our plan has nothing to do with physical force

and leagues offensive and defensive, which at the commencement of the abovementioned councils, leagues, diets, alliances,
and congresses, sowed the seeds of their dissolution; but our
plan depends entirely on the influence of moral power for
the good it will do to the world, but it retains
*73   the * expectation of settling the principles of inter-
national law, by compact and agreement, in a general
treaty, to which the nations of Christendom will be parties;
and it also retains the principle and practice of peaceful
mediation between contending factions or nations, and the
promotion of every plan for bettering the moral, intellectual,
and physical condition of man.

26. In the foregoing plans, the number of delegates from
each of the allied nations has been different at different
unions. The best way, I think, is to allow of as many delegates to the Congress of Nations as any government would
choose to send, but each delegation to be considered as a
separate college, entitled to but one vote, and to but one
turn to speak in the discussions, so as to be considered as but
one person, and if any college should be equally divided on
any question, of course their vote would be neutralized. To
avoid this difficulty, the number in each college might be an
odd one.

*CHAPTER IX.

SOME ACCOUNT OF ATTEMPTS WHICH HAVE BEEN MADE BY
PRIVATE INDIVIDUALS AND PEACE SOCIETIES TO CALL
THE ATTENTION OF THE PUBLIC TO THE SUBJECT
OF A CONGRESS OF NATIONS.

1. WILLIAM PENN in 1693 published an " Essay on the present and future peace of Europe," in which he urged the plan of a general congress for the settlement of international disputes, and referring to the " great design " of Henry IV, he says: " His example tells us that *this is fit to be done.* Sir William Temple's history of the United Provinces shows, by a surpassing instance, that *it may be done,* and Europe, by her incomparable miseries, that *it ought to be done."* * I have read the Essay. It is chiefly remarkable for having been the first thing of the kind in modern times.

2. Charles Castel Irene de Saint Pierre, who died in *75 the year 1743, and who must be distinguished * from the author of the Studies of Nature, who was his nephew, seems to have been the author of the next published dissertation on a Congress of Nations. There is nothing left of this Essay, but a review of it, which is published among

* Herald of Peace.

the works of John James Rousseau. St. Pierre was the originator of the plan, but Rousseau seems to have admired it, and published this review with remarks of his own. The plan of St. Pierre and Rousseau was a confederation, like the Amphictyonic Council, the Helvetic Union, &c. — a system of legislation and arbitration enforced by arms. They adopt the error common to ancient and modern times, that, " It is necessary that no considerable power should refuse." The projector makes five articles necessary to the confederacy. " By the first, the contracting sovereigns should establish among themselves a perpetual and inviolable alliance, appointing plenipotentiaries to hold a fixed and permanent diet, or congress, in a certain place, in which diet, all the differences arising between the contracting parties shall be regulated and decided by way of arbitration." The other four articles show how the decrees of the diet should be enforced by arms; and undertakes to answer some objections. The author then recapitulates the evils attending the settlement of national controversies by war, under thirteen heads, and opposes to them the advantages by arbitration, under eight heads. Both the evils and advantages are too obvious to need particular notice. Saint Pierre presented his scheme to all the monarchs of Europe, and among

* 76   the rest to Louis XV, of France.   * Cardinal Fleury, the prime minister, pleasantly told the author, that " he had forgotten one preliminary article, which was the delegation of missionaries to dispose the hearts of the princes of Europe to submit to such a diet." The peace societies must furnish these missionaries, and send them to the princes in monarchical governments, and to the people in mixed and republican governments. Let public opinion be on our side, and missionaries will not be wanting.

3. The subject of a Congress of Nations seems to have

slept in forgetfulness amid the thunders of the late wars in Europe, when the attention of mankind was so engrossed with plans of mutual destruction, that there was no opportunity for the " still small voice " of peace to be heard. Yet there were a few who thought on the evils of war, and sought a remedy. In the London " Monthly Magazine " of July, 1811, appeared an anonymous letter to the editor, from which I make the following extract: " It appears to me, that if the powerful at the head of different nations would seriously turn their thoughts to the subject, that it is not without some probability, that a *National Court of Arbitration* might be established, to which, when two nations disagree, their cause might be referred; and that the decision of this court would frequently, if not always, be abided by. Do we not see, when a difference exists between two people respecting some transaction in business, that the cause is referred to private arbitration and the decision abided by?

      Why, therefore, would it be impossible to form a
* 77   national court of arbitration? I * rather compare a
      court of this sort to an arbitration than to a court of justice; for in an arbitration, the parties choose their friends to be settlers of the dispute, which is not the case when people go to law; the judge and jury, perhaps, are all unknown to the parties differing. Each nation might send one or more deputies to the National Court, which should, perhaps, meet at different places, as might suit, or have one permanent place of assembling." " P.S. Was there ever an attempt of this kind acted on? " These few thoughts appear to be very crude. The writer does not seem to have been aware of the necessity of a Congress of Nations, previous to a Court of Nations, to organize such a court, define its powers, and prescribe the principles on which it should judge; nor does he seem to be aware, that if " each

nation send one or more deputies to the National Court," it would be impossible and improper for " the parties to choose *their friends,*" to be settlers of a dispute. This writer appears to be ignorant, that any one else ever thought of a Court of Nations; and I never saw his articles until I had arrived at this place in my Essay. Could people be brought together to confer on this plan, nine out of ten of the decent people of Christendom would agree to it, as soon as they understood it.

4. The London Peace Society has always been friendly to the plan of a Court or Congress of Nations, as appears by the following extract from the Herald of Peace, which is their organ. " The Court of Nations is the end of the operations of the peace * societies," but it has never taken any decided action on it, until lately. The Herald of Peace for July, 1839, contains a petition to Parliament on the subject of a Congress of Nations, which was presented on the 12th of April preceding, by Edward Baines, Esq., member for Leeds, and in the House of Lords by I know not who. I mention this event in this place for the purpose of preserving the connection. But as it is best to observe the order of time in the Appendix, I have given this petition the place of No. 13.

*78

5. There is nothing in the publications of the Massachusetts Peace Society which favors the idea that the plan for a Congress of Nations ever engaged the attention of the Rev. Noah Worcester, D. D., the venerable founder of that institution, and the only editor of " Friend of Peace," the organ of that society, or of any one of its members; nor do we find any mention of the plan in the publications or proceedings of any other peace society in America prior to the organization of the American Peace Society.

6. The American Peace Society was organized at a meet-

ing commenced on the 8th of May, 1828, in the city of New York. The following is an extract from the circular letter accepted at that time by the Society, which shows that a Congress of Nations was a prominent object with the founders of it. " We hope to increase and promote the practice already begun, of submitting national differences to amicable discussion and arbitration, and finally of settling all national controversies by an appeal to reason, as be-

comes rational creatures, and not by physical
* 79 force, * as is worthy only of brute beasts, and this
shall be done by a *Congress of Christian Nations,* whose decrees shall be enforced by public opinion, that rules the world; not by public opinion as it now is, but by public opinion when it shall be enlightened by the rays of the gospel of peace." * It is very evident, that the notions of the founders of the American Peace Society were on this subject very crude and undigested, when they sanctioned and published this circular letter. It has been by constantly thinking, writing and speaking, on this subject, for eleven years, that their ideas have got to be more mature; and they now see that a distinction ought to be made between a congress of ambassadors, for the purpose of settling the disputed points of the law of nations, and a court of judges, to decide cases submitted to them by the mutual consent of the parties concerned, — in other words, a distinction between the legislative and the judicial power.

7. At their next anniversary, the American Peace Society offered a premium of thirty dollars, for the best dissertation on a Congress of Nations. Only four or five dissertations were handed in, and all of them of a very ordinary character. One of them, however, which was thought rather superior to the others, with the consent of the author, was published

* Harbinger of Peace, Vol. I, p. 10.

in a double number of the Harbinger of Peace for January and February, 1831, and is believed to be the first dissertation on a Congress of Nations ever published

*80   in * America. I have made copious extracts from it, in writing this Essay. Subsequently the Society offered fifty dollars for the best dissertation on the subject, but with no better success. The premium was too small; but the funds of the Society did not allow them to increase it. The subject was afterwards taken up by two gentlemen of New York, as is related in the preface to the volume of Prize Essays on a Congress of Nations; to which I refer the reader.

8. At the annual meeting of the American Peace Society, held at New York, May 11, 1830, there was laid before the Society a letter from J. P. Blanchard, Esq., Corresponding Secretary of the Massachusetts Peace Society, enclosing an abbreviated copy of a letter to him, from a gentleman of Boston, not a member of any peace society, which abbreviation Mr. Blanchard was directed by the Massachusetts Peace Society, to transmit to the American Peace Society. In this letter, the gentleman informs the Massachusetts Peace Society, through their secretary, that he had penned an instrument, and offered it for signatures, not to the members of the peace societies, — who might have been supposed to have already expressed an opinion on the subject, — but to those who had no connection with them. The following is a copy of the instrument: " We the undersigned, convinced of the great advantages and blessings which *an abolition of war,* and the reference of all international disputes to *a Court of Nations,* would confer on mankind, heartily concur in recommending a suitable

*81   reference of this * subject, by the peace societies, to the attention of Congress, as soon as such a ref-

erence shall be found practicable and convenient." Nine
out of ten, to whom this instrument was presented, signed
it without hesitation, and those who declined signing, generally expressed their approbation of it.

9. The American Peace Society, at the abovementioned
annual meeting, approved of these measures, and directed
the correspondence to be published in the Harbinger of
Peace, which was done.* They entered warmly into the
measure, and struck off a circular containing the proposal,
which was widely circulated among the most intelligent and
influential characters in New England, and it was found
that almost every one to whom the instrument was presented
signed it, amounting, in all, to several thousands of names,
besides some, which from inadvertence or accident, were
never returned. Considerable time, however, elapsed before
the friends of peace thought themselves authorized to solicit
the aid of legislative action — for when an enterprise of
this kind has to be carried on by a few individuals, who
are viewed by the bulk of the community as good-natured
enthusiasts, who are seeking a great and good, but unattainable object, and where the ill health of one of them
causes serious embarrassment, things move slowly. A small
obstacle impedes the ascending wheel. It was not until the
year 1835, that the subject was brought before the
* 82 Legislature of the State * of Massachusetts — a
State, of which it is no disparagement to any other
in the Union to say, goes before all the rest in every good
work. February 6, of this year, a petition,† praying for an
expression of opinion on the subject of a Congress of
Nations, signed only by Thomas Thompson, Jr., and William
Ladd, was presented by the Hon. Sidney Willard to the
Senate, who took the same into consideration, and referred

* Harbinger of Peace, Vol. III, p. 131, and seq.   † Appendix, No. 2.

it to a special committee of three, who made a very able
report,* favorable to the prayer of the petitioners, accompanied with the following resolutions:

"*Resolved,* That in the opinion of this Legislature, some
mode should be established for the amicable and final adjustment of all international disputes, instead of resort to war."

"*Resolved,* That the Governor of this Commonwealth be
requested to communicate a copy of the above report and
of the resolutions annexed, to the Executive of each of the
States, to be laid before the Legislature thereof, inviting a
cooperation for the advancement of the object in view."

This report, with the resolutions appended, was adopted
by the Senate by a majority of 19 to 5, only a very little
having been said against it, by a gentleman, who, needlessly,
acknowledged that he had never examined the subject.
Before this report was made and adopted by the Senate,
it had got to be too late in the session to carry the subject
before the House, and nothing more was done on it,
* 83   in the Legislature * of Massachusetts, this year. The
next year, Mr. Thompson, on whose perseverance and
diligence the cause depended in a great measure for success
with the Legislature of Massachusetts, was confined to his
house by sickness.

10. In 1837, a petition was presented to the Legislature
of Massachusetts, signed only by Mr. Thompson,† and
another, signed by the President and the Executive Committee of the Massachusetts Peace Society.‡ These petitions
were referred to a joint committee of the Senate and House
of Representatives, which committee made a very lengthy
and able report,§ to which resolutions were appended something similar to those appended to the preceding report, but

* Appendix, No. 3.   ‡ Appendix, No. 5.
† Appendix, No. 4.   § Appendix, No. 6.

in addition calling the attention of the Executive of the United States to the subject, and recommending " a negotiation with such other governments, as in its wisdom it may deem proper, with a view to effect so important an arrangement." This report, with the resolves appended, was adopted by the Senate by a majority of 35 to 5, and by the House, without a dissenting vote. The subject was subsequently laid before the Legislatures of Maine and Vermont, but on account of its not being so well understood in those States as in Massachusetts, it has been deferred; but it came very near being favorably received by the Legislature of Vermont, where it was lost by its opponents calling party spirit, that bane of all good, to their aid.

* 84 * 11. The American Peace Society was only waiting for the sanction of the Legislature of Massachusetts, to carry the subject before the Congress of the United States. They were, however, anticipated by the New York Peace Society, that had prepared and sent on a very able petition * to Congress. Instead of getting up a new and separate petition, the American Peace Society heartily cooperated with their brethren of other societies, and the friends of peace in general, in forwarding copies of the same petition. There were presented to the House of Representatives, six petitions of members of the New York Peace Society and others, sent by Origen Bachelor, signed by 608 persons; one from the American Peace Society and others, signed by William Ladd and 539 legal voters in the State of Maine, and generally men of the first respectability; one from Thomas Hough, and 143 other members of the Vermont Peace Society; one from Thomas Thompson, Jr., and 135 members of the Legislature of Massachusetts; in all, 1427 names besides those sent to the Senate, and one signed by

* Appendix, No. 7.

most of the gentlemen of the bar in Augusta, Hallowell, and Gardiner, in Maine, and probably others, of which I have no information. In general, more attention was paid to the respectability, than to the number, of subscribers.

12. On the reception of these petitions by the House of Representatives, Mr. Adams, in a letter to the author, *85 remarks, " On the 22d of March last, I * received your memorial signed by 539 legal voters of the State of Maine, and on the 23d presented it to the House, together with that of Thomas Thompson, Jr., and 134 members of the Legislature of Massachusetts, then in session. A memorial of the same purport had been previously presented by me, signed by Origen Bachelor, and 425 members of the New York Peace Society, and others. At certain periods of the session, I had presented three other petitions of similar character, and Mr. Evans of Maine, and my colleague, Mr. Cushing, had presented others. I moved the reference of the first to a *select committee*. The Chairman of the Committee of Foreign Affairs manifested a strong inclination to have it *laid on the table*. He denied that any proposition for an arbitration of differences had been made by the Mexican government, but was afterwards obliged to acknowledge, in this respect, his mistake. But he moved the reference of the petition to his own committee, and it was so referred. The subsequent petitions on the same subject, including yours, were all referred to the same committee. They were viewed by the majority of the House with great jealousy, as abolition petitions, or petitions against the annexation of Texas, in disguise." * The petition was also pre-

* The following are extracts from a letter from ex-president Adams to the Corresponding Secretary of the New York Peace Society:

" Your petition first brought to the notice of the whole government of these United States the *fact*, that the Mexican Congress had, by a solemn decree of the 20th of May, 1837, authorized their Executive to agree with our government

* 86   sented and * advocated in the Senate by Mr. Clay, and ordered to be printed, but there was not sufficient time to act on it, as the session was near its close, and probably the Senate waited for the action of the House, in which body the petitions were referred to the Committee of Foreign Affairs, according to the request of its chairman.

13. The report * of the Committee of Foreign Affairs shows how little our popular men understand the subject. They will understand it better, when it becomes more popular. When we consider the treatment which the

* 87   first motion for the abolition of * the slave trade met with in the British Parliament in 1776 — that there was not one member who had moral courage enough to second the motion, and that the same body afterward, not only abolished the slave trade, but slavery, also, in the

to refer the differences between the two countries to an arbitrator. It appeared at first, that neither the President of the United States, nor their Secretary of State, nor their Chairman of the Committee of Foreign Relations of their House of Representatives, knew the existence of the Mexican decree. It was to your petitions that Congress were indebted for the knowledge that the Mexican decree existed.

"The proposal of a reference to arbitration was itself so reasonable, that no voice was heard in Congress against it. The denial of its existence produced an immediate formal communication of it to the Executive Administration of the United States; and very soon afterwards, it was conditionally accepted. This removed all immediate danger of a war with Mexico; and if the petitioners of the peace societies had never rendered to their country any other service, they would have deserved the thanks of the whole nation for this.

"The other proposals of your petition, urging upon the Congress and government of the United States a course of policy looking to the promotion of universal peace, and for that purpose to the formation and establishment of a Congress of Nations, have been duly considered by the Committee of Foreign Relations, and they have submitted to the House a report, ten thousand copies of which have been ordered to be printed. The close of the present session of Congress is so near, that there will not probably be time for a discussion in the House on its principles."

* Appendix, No. 8.

British West Indies, we have great reason to hope for results equally favorable.

14. Not at all discouraged by a result which they had expected, the American Peace Society forwarded another petition * to the Congress of 1838-9, in which they refute the reasoning of the Committee of Foreign Affairs. The New York Peace Society also sent another petition for a like purpose.† The president of the American Peace Society also took a journey to Washington to attend to the furtherance of this business, and had a special interview with the President of the United States, and conversed with some of the leading members of Congress, from all of whom he gathered, what indeed he knew before, that if the rulers in representative governments are to be induced to adopt any new measure of public utility, it must be through their constituents. In such purposes application must always be made chiefly to those in whom the sovereignty is established, — to monarchs in monarchical governments, to the people in popular governments, and to both in mixed governments. The chief use of such petitions in popular governments is, to bring the subject before the people by means of their representatives. President * 88 Van * Buren said he had noticed the report of the committee of the Legislature of Massachusetts, which had been sent to him, and had read a *part* of it, but had not yet communicated it to Congress. Before either the President or the Congress of these United States will act on this subject, the sovereign people must act, and before they will act, they must be acted on by the friends of peace; and the subject must be laid before the people, in all parts of our country, as much as it has been in Massachusetts, where there has, probably, been as much said and done, on

* Appendix, No. 9.   † Appendix, No. 10.

the subject, as in all the other twenty-five states of the Union. When the whole country shall understand the subject as well as the State of Massachusetts, the Congress of the United States will be as favorable to a Congress of Nations as the General Court of Massachusetts; and when the American government shall take up the subject in earnest, it will begin to be studied and understood by the enlightened nations of Europe. As the session of 1838-9 was what is generally called the short session, closing on the 4th of March, no report was made on these petitions, which, as usual, had been committed to the Committee on Foreign Affairs. Uncertain what would be the fate of these petitions, the American Peace Society thought best to forward another short petition.* Since that petition was sent on, we have learned, through the medium of the public journals,

that the petitions not acted on during the session

* 89   of * 1838-9 are continued in the same committees to

whom they were referred, to be acted on this year [1839-40]. Beside these petitions, shorter ones, signed by many persons, have also been sent on much more numerously this year than ever before.† Very able petitions have also been penned by private individuals, and signed by almost all the citizens of the neighboring community.

15. The attention paid to the subject in Great Britain, and the petition to parliament, we have noticed before.‡ It has also received some attention on the continent of Europe, particularly in Switzerland. The late Count de Sellon, member of the Sovereign Council of Geneva, the founder and president of the peace society of that canton, offered a prize of 400 francs for the best dissertation on this subject,

* Appendix, No. 11.
† For a sample of these petitions, see Appendix, No. 12.
‡ Appendix, No. 13.

in the year 1830, and had some correspondence with the rulers of Europe on the general subject of peace, which was politely and favorably answered; but so extremely difficult is the communication between this country and Switzerland, that we are much in the dark concerning his movements. The time will come, when a Congress of Nations will establish an international post-office for the whole civilized world. Then all the great moral enterprises will move on with an accelerated velocity.

*CHAPTER X.

ON THE OBJECTIONS WHICH MAY BE RAISED AGAINST A CONGRESS AND COURT OF NATIONS.

1. Objections expected—2. Concentration of power—3. No power to enforce the decrees of the Court—4. Danger to governments—5. Danger to republics—6. The present mode of umpirage sufficient—7. Expense—8. The same objections lie against all national arbitration.

1. It is but reasonable to expect objections against our plan. The greater part of the world are opposed to innovations, and consider " an old error better than a new truth." It is much easier to remain in error than to attempt improvement. It requires no effort to keep still, but it does to advance. Hence the progress of moral reformation is always slow. Mankind are apt to cry like the slothful man in the proverb, " There is a lion in the way." But we should not be discouraged for all this, for we know that many things have been accomplished which were once thought as impracticable as the plan which we propose; but we should patiently continue to remove objections as fast as they are brought up. It is probable that similar objections were started when it was first proposed that the trial by jury should take the place of the ordeal of battle, as this had taken the place of private revenge, assassination, and murder. The plan, * 91 which we propose in a Congress of Nations, * is a similar advance on the manners of the age, that the trial by fair battle, regulated by well-known and acknowledged laws, was on the private revenge of the time of Alfred the great; and the Court of Nations substitutes

an appeal to reason for the trial by battle, or an appeal to brute force, as the trial by jury succeeded the ordeal of battle.

2. The first objection, raised by those who have never looked into the subject — which class, unfortunately, comprises the bulk of community — is, that we are for *concentrating too much power in the hands of a few men,* and they fancy great fleets and armies, as was proposed in the Great Scheme of Henry IV. It is a sufficient answer to this objection, that physical power to enforce the laws of our Congress, or the decrees of our Court, forms no part of our plan.

3. The next objection which we shall consider is of quite the contrary character. It is objected, that *we have made no provision for enforcing the laws of our Congress and the decrees of our Court by physical power,* fleets and armies; and that, therefore, such laws and judgments would prove entirely abortive. This objection is somewhat specious and requires consideration. If it be valid, why have so many wise and able writers taken great pains to compose treatises on the Law of Nations. None of these writers possessed the physical power to carry their laws into effect; yet their opinions have always had great weight, and they have been considered benefactors to mankind. Now, should a great number of able civilians convene for the purpose of *92   discussing the * various points of international law, is it not likely, that they would much better express what is the general will of mankind than isolated individuals shut up in their studies? "Law is the expression of the general will," and nothing else, whether it be national or international. There is one great advantage which would attend a Congress of Nations, which is, that on such points as are difficult to settle by abstract reasoning, the representa-

tives of nations could agree in the spirit of *compromise*. The same objection would lie against a weak power ever making a treaty with a strong one. All these laws would be but a treaty, by which the nations represented would bind themselves to observe certain principles, in their future intercourse with one another, both in peace and in war. The same objection would lie against leaving *any* dispute to arbitrators; for no person expects that the umpire will enforce his award by military power. I believe that, even now, *public opinion* is amply sufficient to enforce all the decisions of a Court of Nations, and the " schoolmaster is abroad," and public opinion is daily obtaining more power. If an Alexander, a Cæsar, a Napoleon, have bowed down to public opinion, what may we not expect of better men, when public opinion becomes more enlightened? The *pen* is soon to take the place of the *sword,* and reason is soon to be substituted for brute force, in settling all international controversies. Already there is no civilized nation that can withstand the frown of public opinion. It is therefore necessary, only to enlighten public opinion still
* 93   farther, to insure the * success of our plan. In civilized countries there is not probably one tenth part of the people who obey the laws from fear of the sword of the magistrate. Nine persons out of ten fear disgrace more than they do any other punishment; and men often inflict capital punishment on themselves, in order to escape from the frown of public opinion, which they fear more than death. It is true that, heretofore, public opinion has not had so much influence on nations as on individuals; but, as intercourse between nations increases, the power of public opinion will increase. Nations make war as individuals fight duels, from fear of disgrace, more than from any other cause. If it were disgraceful to go to war when there is a regular way of

obtaining satisfaction without, wars would be as rare as duels in New England, where they are disgraceful.

4. Another objection is, that a *Congress of Nations would be dangerous to existing forms of government,* particularly to the republican form. This objection has been urged with considerable plausibility in this country; but on examination into our plan, it vanishes of itself. The Congress of Nations is not to concern itself with *internal* affairs of nations, but only with *international* affairs, and could have nothing to do with forms of government. Besides, no member of the confederation is bound by any law which it has not ratified; and as each law is of the nature of an article of a treaty, if supposed to be dangerous to free institutions, the delegates from free governments would not vote for it, and * 94   no law can be enacted by the * Congress of Nations without an unanimous vote; and even if it were passed, if it were not ratified by all the nations of the confederacy, it would be null and void, like an article of an unratified treaty. And, again, as the Congress of Nations is not trusted with any physical force, as has been the case with many of the confederacies which we have examined, and was to have been the case in the Great Scheme of Henry IV, there could be no danger of a nation being compelled to change its form of government. And yet, again, the same argument would be equally conclusive against any treaty between a republic and a monarchy.

5. But still the objector urges that, *as the decrees of the Court of Nations are passed by a majority of the judges, as in the Supreme Court of the United States, and not by unanimous consent, as in the Congress of Nations, republics would not stand so good a chance of obtaining justice as monarchies,* which would be more numerously represented in the Court of Nations, and the judges representing them

might be influenced by their prejudices against republics. To this we answer, that it is not certain that monarchies *would* be more numerously represented than republics and limited monarchies; that the United States, a republican government, has been willing to leave its disputes with the crowned heads of Europe, to other crowned heads, without the fear of partiality, and have not suffered by it. The same objection might, with equal plausibility, be urged against a

trial by jury, in which the cause of a catholic may be * 95   tried by a jury of which a majority * are protestants, or a person of one political party by a jury of which a majority are of the opposite party. We do not pretend that our system is perfect, for there is nothing perfect on earth. All that we contend for is, that this peaceful mode of settling international controversies is better than war, and more likely to give a righteous verdict without the innumerable evils of war.

6. It has been objected, *that we have now many precedents of submitting national difficulties to umpires agreed on by both parties, and we want nothing more.* It is true, such references of international difficulties have often taken place of late, and we hail them as auspicious tokens that our plan will finally succeed; for they are very evident approximations to it. But the advantages of a Court of Nations over individual umpirage must be very evident, from the following considerations: 1st. An umpire has *now* no law of nations by which to regulate his decisions. It is granted that there have been many able writers on the law of nations; but their laws are sanctioned by no authority, and they do not agree among themselves. The decisions of individual umpires would be formed by no rule of generally acknowledged law; and would often be different under similar circumstances; which would not only detract from their moral power, but

would prevent the formation of a body of international common law, to be a guide to future decisions.   2d. A single umpire, especially a crowned head, having political and commercial relations to all the rest of the world,

* 96   cannot be expected * to be so impartial as a bench of eminent jurists, selected from the most renowned in their own country for their talents, integrity and experience, and translated from the highest judicial stations in their own nation to fill the highest judicial station in the world; especially as they know that their judgments will be rejudged by all mankind, and to the latest posterity. With such men, the desire of a reputation for being great jurists has been their ruling passion through life — their ultimate object; and a stronger motive could not be laid before them. They may err in judgment, for " to err is human," but they would not be so likely to err as a single umpire, and bribing would be out of the question; and if one could possibly be bribed, the majority of them could not. 3d. Such men are not only more able than men in general to detect the sophisms and false reasoning of the pleaders of either party to an international dispute, but they are more able to make the case plain to all the world. It is of little importance for a judge to be able to perceive the truth, if he is not able to make the truth appear plain to the jury, not only as to matters of fact, but also as to matters of argument. No one who has been in the habit of attending common courts of law is unconscious of something like this, in his own mind. One barrister gets up and pleads the cause of his client; and the unpractised juryman thinks that the truth is undoubtedly with him. The counsel for the opposite party pleads, and then the juryman reverses his decision, or hangs in doubt. But the judge takes up the case, strips

* 97   the * falsehood from the truth, and exposes the

sophistry of the pleaders; and then the jury unanimously agree upon a verdict. 4th. Experience shows how much nations prefer a numerous body of umpires to a single one. Within the last two hundred years there have been fifty congresses for the settlement of international difficulties, though there have not been ten cases of individual umpirage in the same time. Had there been a Court of Nations, the French government would, probably, have submitted its disputes with Mexico, Buenos Ayres, and, perhaps, with queen Pomare, also, to it, instead of deciding them by the mouth of the cannon; for, in answer to the offer of England to mediate between France and Mexico, the French government, through its official organ, the Journal des Debats, replied: " No foreign tribunal is *sufficiently elevated* to impose its jurisdiction " in the premises. These remarks were considered by the court of London as coming from an official source, and they contain a precious confession, on the part of France, that there is great need of such a tribunal as the Court of Nations, which would be " sufficiently elevated " to judge this and similar cases.

7. Some may be disposed to object to our plan, *on account of its expense*. This would be light indeed when compared with the cost of war. It would not cost a nation so much as the maintenance of a single gun-boat, nor all Christendom so much as the support of a single frigate in active service; while it would save thousands of millions, * 98   pay off the national debts * of all countries, reduce the taxes seven-eighths, and leave a large fund for internal improvements, education, and every useful work.

8. We may, therefore, safely *conclude,* that no objection can be brought against our plan of a Congress and Court of Nations, which is not equally valid against all legislative and judicial bodies; that the system is safe for all forms of

government; that its expense is not worth naming; and that it is altogether preferable to individual umpirage, as it concentrates the public opinion of the whole civilized world, and would be able to enforce its decrees and decisions by moral power alone.

*C H A P T E R X I.

THE REASONS WHICH WE HAVE TO HOPE THAT A CONGRESS AND COURT OF NATIONS MAY BE, BEFORE LONG, ESTABLISHED.

1. Every thing which ought to be done can be done—2. Great changes have taken place—3. Individual vengeance of former times—4. Origin and progress of society—5. Change of opinion in religious persecution—6. On piracy— 7. On war—8. Amelioration of the evils of war—9. Religious wars no longer tolerated—10. Opinion on the slave trade changed—11. Also on the use of alcohol—12. Improvements in civil society—13. Increased power of public opinion—14. Increased intercourse of nations—15. Missionary enterprise— 16. Disposition to arbitrate international difficulties—17. Improvement in the arts of destruction—18. The ascending side of justice—19. Favorable principle in human nature—20. Prophecy.

1. IT is an incontrovertible axiom, that *every thing of a moral nature which ought to be done, can be done.* There is no object favorable to the happiness of mankind, and founded on the immutable principles of truth, which zeal, intelligence and perseverance, with self-sacrifice, will not finally accomplish. I do not say that so great an enterprise, as a Congress of Nations, can be accomplished in a day. It will probably be of slow growth, like the trial by jury, and by slow degrees it will ultimately arrive at the same approximation to perfection, which that has arrived at. There is the greater need, therefore, that those who favor the object should begin the work without loss of time. * 100 If we wish to eat of the date, we should * plant the seed immediately. If we wish our children to see the flower of the aloe, we must ourselves begin the cultivation.

2. If we look back into the history of the world, we shall

have no reason to doubt the truth of the abovementioned axiom; for changes have taken place in the world as wonderful as would be the change from the trial of international disputes by brute force and the chance of war, to the trial of such disputes by reason and an impartial tribunal. Indeed, such changes have already taken place with respect to individuals, and even of independent states confederated together for the purpose, though on a small scale. I shall briefly allude to a few of these changes.

3. The time was, when every individual took vengeance into his own hands, as nations do now. Even among the chosen people of God, the avenger of blood was allowed to pursue the manslayer, and if he overtook the homicide before he reached a city of refuge, he slew him without a trial. This practice, but without the city of refuge, still obtains among the savage nations of America, the Arabs, and in many parts of Greece. When, therefore, Alfred the great instituted the ordeal by battle and regulated revenge by law and gave it the sanction of religion, it was considered a great advance on the barbarous manners of the age. Bringing the custom of war — which is nothing else than the custom of unregulated robbery, revenge and assassination — under certain rules and regulations, avoiding much of its frequency, abating its cruelty, and diminishing the number of
* 101 persons * who should be considered combatants, would prepare the way for subjecting the whole system to a trial by reason and the Court of Nations, as the ordeal by battle was gradually changed into the Grand Assize, which was substituted for it by St. Louis, of France, and Henry II, of England, after an existence of five centuries. This amelioration began by exempting certain *characters* from the trial by battle; then certain *causes* were excluded; then other causes, *under certain circumstances,* as when compurgators,

or jurors, would swear to the innocence of the accused, — but the juror was liable to be challenged by the prosecutor, — the accused could not be compelled to *risk life or limb a second time,* under the same accusation, and many other ameliorations were gradually introduced, until the judicial combat became entirely obsolete in all countries where it had existed; and the only shadow of it left is the modern duel, though it has not been ten years, since the trial by battle, in all cases, was formally expunged from the statute law of England. Formerly, the judicial combat was almost universal in Christendom, and was impiously called an " appeal to heaven," and was preceded by fasting and prayer, as the custom of war is now. If this custom of the duel or private war, once sanctioned by church and state, has been denounced by both, why may not the custom of war, in due time, share the same fate?

4. The origin and progress of society also affords a hope, that a trial of international disputes by a regularly constituted court, judging by known and acknowledged * 102 laws, may in time take the place of * the ordeal of war. Small bodies, like the independent states of Greece, Italy, Germany, Gaul, the Saxon Heptarchy, the Hanse Towns, the Helvetic Union, &c., have voluntarily congregated together, not only for the purpose of mutual defence against a foreign power, but for mutual defence against each other. These found it necessary to constitute certain councils and diets, which were as successful in securing peace among the several members of the league, as could reasonably have been expected, considering the darkness, ignorance, and belligerent spirit of the times in which they existed; and were bright spots in the history of those dark ages. But they admitted two principles among them, which destroyed, at length, their utility, and from which our plan

is free. The first of these was, the enforcement of their decrees by the power of the sword, instead of depending on moral power alone. The other evil, which attended their organizations, was the union of the legislative, judiciary and executive powers in one body. This introduced intrigue, ambition, and many other baleful passions and practices, which strongly tried their principles of peace and justice; but with all these disadvantages, — such is the force of the principles which we advocate, — they continued to preserve peace among themselves for centuries, with but little interruption; and when they fell, they fell rather by external violence than internal dissensions.

5. The change of opinion on the necessity of religious persecution warrants the hope, that it will likewise * 103 change on the necessity of war. There was * a time when religious persecution was thought as necessary to the safety of the church as war is now to the safety of the state; and this opinion was peculiar to no sect, for Protestants were persecutors as well as Catholics. The fires of persecution were lighted up in all parts of the Christian world, and rivers of blood flowed, for the vain purpose of procuring an uniformity of faith and practice in the affairs of religion; but who now would dare to raise his voice in favor of religious persecution? If so wonderful a change in public opinion has taken place with respect to religious wars, why may we not expect a similar change with respect to political wars?

6. Piracy was practised and honored by the polished Athenians, who plundered and enslaved all who were not Greeks; and piracy has been allowed, and even honored, almost to the present day. Sir Thomas Cavendish, a famous pirate, flourished about the year 1590, and the celebrated Dampiere, about a century later. The latter was advanced

to the command of the sloop of war Roebuck. Charles II knighted Morgan, a famous pirate, and gave him the command of one of his ships of war. Now who is there to advocate piracy? It is true, privateering is but licensed piracy, and we can hardly conceive the difference between the unlicensed pirate and the foreigner who ships on board a privateer, to fight against a country with which his own is at peace, and to rob and murder those who never injured him or his country. The time is not far distant when, though war may be continued, such men will be * 104 treated * as pirates, and the whole system of privateering abandoned by the mutual consent of all civilized nations, assembled by their ambassadors in a Congress of Nations.

7. The great change which has lately taken place in public opinion, on the lawfulness and expediency of war, affords a hope that this change will go on, until the time shall come when it will be thought neither glorious, just, nor wise, to conquer foreign countries, and thereby load the conquering country with debts and taxes, as well as the conquered nation. Once it was different. Lord Bacon was of opinion, that war was as necessary to the welfare of the state, as exercise to the health of a man. Hobbes maintained that there was no obligation of justice between nations; and that wars for conquest and spoil were authorized by the law of nature. Fenelon, the amiable archbishop of Cambray, in his Telemachus, advises his prince to send his subjects into foreign wars, to acquire a martial spirit and disseminate it among their countrymen. But Frederic the great, though a great conqueror, considered that no conquest he ever made was worth one year's interest of the money it cost. Franklin thought that there never was a good war, nor a bad peace. Jefferson was an honorary member of the Massachusetts

Peace Society, and so was the emperor Alexander. Cassimir Perrier, the late lamented prime minister of France, was eminently a man of peace, and so is Lord Brougham, and even Daniel O'Connell. This change of opinion, on the subject of war, indicates that a change of measures is not far distant in the vista of time.

* 105   * 8. The amelioration of the physical evils and sufferings of war warrants a belief, that they may be further ameliorated, until war comes to be attenuated to a mere shadow of what it has been. It may be true that " the natural state of man is war," as was affirmed by Hobbes; but Christianity has begun to modify the natural state of man, and its first step was a mitigation of the horrors of war. Formerly, poison and assassination were practised by civilized nations, as they are still by barbarians. Christianity has abolished those customs. But Christian nations still starve their enemies in masses, and assassinate them by wholesale. Formerly, all the inhabitants of an enemy's country were treated alike, and were enslaved or killed. Now, the greater part are considered as non-combatants, and their life and liberty are spared; and there is reason to hope that this list of non-combatants will be farther enlarged, so as to embrace all men following their peaceful business, whether by sea or land. Formerly, all the property of the enemy was considered lawful prize to the captor. Now, private property *on shore* is respected; and we have reason to hope, that this amelioration will advance, until private property shall be respected on the ocean, at least under a neutral flag. Why may not these ameliorations continue to go on, until war becomes a mere matter of form and nonintercourse?

9. There are many things which were formerly thought justifiable causes of war, which are thought so no longer. Once it was thought right to propagate Christianity by

* 106 the sword! Crusades were preached * up, not only
          against the pagans, but against various sects of Chris-
tians, and they were thought agreeable to justice and the
gospel of the Prince of peace. Once, wars for conquest and
spoil were justified, and conquerors extolled to the skies and
almost deified. Now, public opinion is so far corrected, that
wars to propagate the Christian religion are never thought
of, and wars for conquest and plunder are reprobated, and
those who engage in them are compelled, by the power of
public opinion, to issue a manifesto to show the justice of
their cause; for men now fight *professedly* for justice. A
little more light will show mankind that the sword is a capri-
cious arbiter of justice; and were there an adequate tribunal,
no government could without disgrace appeal to the sword
for justice, at least, until it had invited its adversary to refer
their disputes to that tribunal. Nations are now not justified
in resorting to war, until they have tried every other mode of
redress; and war is called " the last resort of kings," simply
because there never has been an international tribunal on an
extended scale.

10. The great change in public opinion which has taken
place with respect to the slave trade, warrants the hope,
that a similar change may take place with respect to war.
This trade was carried on for centuries, with the approbation
of the Christian public; and millions of our fellow-creatures
have been carried into hopeless bondage. Yet it was not
until the year 1776, that any attempt was made to abolish
          it; and that attempt was met with a more decided
* 107 rejection, * by the British parliament, than our peti-
          tions for a Congress of Nations have met with from
the American congress. The advocates of the abolition of
the slave trade were then treated with greater contempt than
the advocates of the abolition of war are now. Yet the

former succeeded beyond their most sanguine expectations, and similar success may attend the advocates of peace.

11. The great change in public opinion, which has taken place with respect to the benefit to be derived from the use of ardent spirits, warrants a hope, that a similar change will take place at no distant day, with respect to the utility of war. Once, alcohol was thought as necessary to the health of a man, as war is now to the safety of the state; but alcohol is now denounced as poison, and the time is not far distant when war will be considered a greater evil than alcohol. Not long since, the advocates of total abstinence from all that can intoxicate, were considered fanatics; but their wonderful success shows the power of truth when properly presented. Many, who once considered the trade in ardent spirits lawful, have now abandoned it. The same may take place with respect to the trade of war.

12. The improvements in *civil society,* which have been increasing since the last great war in Europe, in a geometrical ratio, warrant the belief, that mankind will adopt a more rational and civilized mode of settling their disputes than the barbarous custom of war. Arms have, in a great measure, given place to laws. Formerly, a man had no
* 108 other way of acquiring * celebrity, than being great in fight, and in emulating savage beasts in the display of courage and ferocity. The arts, the sciences, politics, jurisprudence, travels, inventions, and the benevolent enterprises of the day, furnish more rational fields for the ambitious. Emulation in the works of benevolence is taking place of emulation in the arts of destruction.

13. The late improvement in, and increased power of, *public opinion* furnish another guaranty of peace. Glory and conquest are no longer acknowledged as justifiable causes of war. Every war requires a manifesto in which

the justification of war measures is attempted. Even Napoleon himself, in the plenitude of his power, trembled at the shaking of a pen, in the hand of a British reviewer. No army, no fortress, can withstand the attacks of public opinion. It reaches the tyrant on the throne, and the conqueror on the field of battle, and stings through the folds of purple and the coat of mail. "Arms cannot kill it. It is invulnerable, and, like Milton's angels, 'Vital in every part, it cannot, but by annihilation, die.' " * Public opinion is daily becoming more powerful, because more enlightened; for " great is the truth, and it will prevail," and finally triumph for ever over brute force.

14. The increased intercourse of nations is another guaranty of peace. It was the former policy of nations to be as independent of one another as possible — withdraw-
* 109 ing within themselves like a tortoise, to * look on security from external danger as the chief end of government; without exchanging the gifts of kind Providence with other nations, by means of that great highway, the ocean, which he has created for the purpose of exchanging the surplus products of one nation for the superfluities of another; and thus relieving the necessities of all. Under this Chinese system, mankind became prejudiced, morose and misanthropic, and considered the depression of a neighboring country the elevation of their own. Nations now begin to see, that God has made mankind for a system of mutual dependence on one another, and that the more we are dependent on another nation, the more that nation is dependent on us — that to impoverish our customers is not to enrich ourselves, and that the more we buy of other nations, the more they will buy of us. Hence a wonderful spring has been given to commerce — all climates are brought into

* D. Webster.

juxtaposition, and the superfluities of one climate minister to the wants, the comforts, and the luxuries of another. This happy state of things is interrupted by war; and the evils of war are found not only in the tax-book of the belligerent, but in the workshop, and on the farm and plantation of the neutral. The manufacturers and merchants of England would have found their advantage in paying all the claims of France on Mexico, if that would have prevented the blockade of La Vera Cruz. Though the United States were almost the only carriers in the world, during the late wars in Europe, yet they found their commerce so crippled * 110 and * restricted by war, that they preferred a state of war itself to neutrality. The world has at length found out, that it is for the interest of every nation to keep all the other nations at peace.

15. The union of almost all Christian nations in spreading the gospel of peace over the world, is another of the signs of the times favorable to the cause of permanent and universal peace. In the dark ages, Christian nations united in arms, and bishop-generals led their mailed monks and vassals to Palestine, for the purpose of wresting an empty sepulchre from the hands of the infidels, by sword and spear. In the words of Anna Comnena, " All Europe was emptied on Asia." They took the sword, and they perished by the sword. Now, an holier enterprise is on foot, more consistent with the genius of Christianity. Christians have again gone forth, but armed with the " sword of the Spirit, which is the word of God; " and their design is to conquer the world and to bring it under the mild sceptre of the Prince of peace; and every wind brings us news of their success in one quarter or another. War would put a stop to all these peaceful conquests, not only by stopping all intercourse, but by a still worse consequence — the example of fighting Christians on

those they are seeking to convert to the gospel of peace. With what reluctance must the missionaries inform the new converts, that their stations must be abandoned, because the Christian nations, that had ministered to their support, were engaged in mutual slaughter! Every one who sup-
* 111 ports the missionary * cause will, if consistent, favor the cause of peace and a Congress of Nations.

16. A disposition among the nations of Christendom to mediate and to arbitrate, is another of the signs of the times, which is highly auspicious to the cause of permanent and universal peace. Never, before, was there such a disposition to avoid war. Belgium and Holland have referred their disputes to England and France. Great Britain and America have referred their disputes to Russia and Holland. The United States and Mexico have called on the king of Prussia as an umpire between them; and the benevolent exertions of Christian nations have extended beyond Christendom, and the five great powers of Europe have offered to mediate between the Grand Sultan and the Pacha of Egypt. This is indeed the " era of good feelings; " and the time is at hand, when no nation will venture on war before an offer of arbitration, without disgrace bordering on execration. Now, if the arbitration of an individual umpire is good, the judgment of a regular Court of Nations is better, for the reason already shown; so that there can be no reasonable doubt, that such a court will, ere-long, be established.

17. Even the late improvement in the arts of destruction, and the increased expense of war, are a security for the continuance of peace. It is true, many of the barbarous and protracted torments of ancient warfare, such as poison, and the starvation and crucifixion of prisoners have ceased among Christians, but the means of immediate de-
* 112 struction have greatly * increased. The congreve-

rocket, the torpedo, the newly invented bomb and bul-
let, the steam-frigate, and many others in contemplation,
afford means of immediate destruction unknown to the
ancients, or to modern nations not yet converted to Christianity; and they enable the machinist to be more efficient
in destroying human life than the hero.　The increased
expense of carrying on war by these terrible engines, rather
than by human machines, will occasion a great increase of
the burthens of war, and will make it more difficult to raise
the requisite amount of taxes; and this will turn the attention,
both of rulers and subjects, to a cheaper method of settling
international disputes.

18. The ascending scale of justice, from the mayor's or
justice's courts, to the inferior and the superior courts, and
finally to the Supreme Court of the United States, wants
but one step more to complete the system, and that is a
court which shall settle disputes between sovereign and independent nations in the same manner as the Supreme Court
of the United States has settled many cases of disputes
between the several sovereign and independent States of
North America, without ever yet having caused the shedding
of one drop of blood.　The Admiralty court of Great Britain
affects to be a court of appeals to decide cases between the
British government and foreigners, by the law of nations,
when not restrained by acts of parliament; but it is not
independent, nor is its authority acknowledged out of the
British empire.　The several diets of the various confederations of Europe are humble imitations of a Court of
* 113　Nations, in reference to the members of * the confederacy by which they have been organized.　Only one
step further and we have a Court of Nations.　There is great
reason to hope, that this step will ere-long be taken, and the
scale of justice completed.

19. There is one general principle of human nature, which ought not to be left out of our account, and that is, that when men meet together with a sincere desire of doing any thing which ought to be done, that very desire and that very meeting are guaranties that the thing they contemplate will be done. Now if a convention of delegates from the chief powers of Christendom should meet together, with a sincere desire to organize a Congress and Court of Nations, it is absurd to suppose they cannot do it.

20. The above arguments and facts which go to show that the time is near when Christian and civilized nations will seek some other arbiter than the sword to settle their disputes, are amply sufficient to convince any unprejudiced mind of the practicability of the plan which we propose. But as I am writing for those nations that profess to believe in the divine inspiration of the Holy Scriptures, I draw my concluding argument from them. From the many prophecies which predict a time of permanent and universal peace, I select only one. " But in the last days, it shall come to pass, that the mountain of the house of the Lord shall be established in the top of the mountains, and it shall be exalted above the hills; and people shall flow unto it. And many nations shall come, and say, Come, and let us go up to the mountain of the Lord, and to the house of * 114 the God * of Jacob; and he will teach us of his ways, and we will walk in his paths; for the law shall go forth of Zion, and the word of the Lord from Jerusalem. And he shall judge among many people, and rebuke strong nations afar off; and they shall beat their swords into plough-shares, and their spears into pruning-hooks: nation shall not lift up a sword against nation, neither shall they *learn* war any more. But they shall sit, every man under his vine and under his fig-tree; and none shall make them afraid: *for the*

mouth of the Lord of hosts hath spoken it." Micah 4: 1—4. Now, though we may reasonably expect, from the promises of God, and the signs of the times, that the period is not far distant, when wars will cease; yet we cannot reasonably expect, that while man remains the same selfish creature he is, disputes and contentions will altogether cease; but that very selfishness will induce him to seek some cheaper, safer and surer way of obtaining justice, than war; and a Court of Nations will be both the cause and effect of the perpetual cessation of war. Mankind have tried war long enough to know that it seldom redresses grievances, and that it generally costs more than the redress is worth, even when it is most successful; and " that," to use the words of Jefferson, " war is an instrument entirely inefficient toward redressing wrong; that it multiplies instead of indemnifying losses." What, then, shall hinder the nations from adopting a cheap and sure mode of redress, such as a Court of Nations promises? — what but blindness to their own happiness, which cannot always endure?

*CHAPTER XII.

ON THE BENEFITS WHICH WOULD BE LIKELY TO ACCRUE FROM
A CONGRESS AND A COURT OF NATIONS.

1. Little need be said under this head—2. Code of international law—3. Court
of Nations—4. Conservators of the peace of nations—5. Abatement of taxation—6. Saving of human life—7. Moral evils of war prevented.

1. MUCH need not be said on this subject after the preceding chapters, as it would be only a repetition of arguments. In fact, the advantages are so obvious, that it is
not necessary to say much; but I will mention a few particulars not before stated, or but slightly alluded to.

2. One advantage to be derived from a Congress of Nations is a code of international law, no longer dependent
on the conflicting and changing opinions of civilians, but
solemnly agreed upon, after mature deliberation, by the
nations represented by their wisest men, and confirmed by
the respective governments, like a treaty of peace or commerce. Every nation, every independent state, every city
and body corporate, nay, even every voluntary association,
thinks it necessary to have a well-defined code of laws, by
which to regulate their conduct with one another. Why,
then, should not the community of nations have such
* 116 a code of laws, mutually agreed on * and promulgated,
so as to be read and known by all men?

3. If it is necessary to have such a code of laws, it is no
less necessary to have an independent body of men, authorized and commissioned to interpret those laws, instead of
leaving every state to make that interpretation which suits
its own interest.

4. It would be a great advantage to the world, to have a respectable body of men to act as conservators of the peace of nations, whose office it should be, when they saw a war brewing between any two nations, to offer their mediation, and propose terms of compromise. Often a nation, like an individual, goes to war for honor, when she would be very glad to refrain, were it not from fear that her courage or her power would be suspected. In such cases, a mediator, like the Court of Nations, would generally keep the peace of nations.

5. Submission of international disputes to a Court of Nations would relieve the people of most nations of seven-eighths of their taxes. It is computed that 750,000,000 of dollars are annually drawn from the pockets of the people of Europe, for the purposes of keeping up war-establishments in time of peace; nearly all of which could be spared, and either left for the increased enjoyments of all classes of community, or expended in internal improvements, or in common schools, academies and colleges. If the governments of Europe would adopt the measure of a simultaneous disarmament, they might do it without fear, and spend the sums, now lavished on armies, in * 117 increasing the * comforts and education of the poor, for then, they would have no occasion for standing armies to keep the people in subjection; and the wealth so expended would soon be returned to government, with interest, from the increased ability of their subjects to pay taxes, and the increased ability of all classes of the people to purchase the luxuries of life, which might still be sufficiently taxed, while the necessaries of life might be left free from taxation.

6. The saving of money, now lavished in supporting stupendous naval and military establishments, would be of small

consideration, when compared with the saving of human life, by a pacific policy. It is supposed that the average life of a soldier in war does not exceed three years. The celebrated Neckar calculated, that one third of new recruits perished the first year by the hardships of a military life. Of the victims of war, probably not one in ten ever feels the stroke of an enemy. Who can tell the amount of physical suffering endured in war, when the most civilized nations of the world bend all their ingenuity, arts, and knowledge to the single purpose of inflicting the greatest possible amount of suffering on one another?

7. But the physical evils and pains of war are " trifles light as air," when compared with its moral evils, and the contamination of the fleet and the camp, " where," as Dr. Doddridge says, in his Life of Colonel Gardiner, " the temptations are so many, and the prevalence of the vicious character so great, that it may seem no inconsiderable

* 118   praise and felicity, to be * free from dissolute vice; and the few who do escape, should be recorded heroes indeed, and highly favored of Heaven." The celebrated Robert Hall, in a sermon against war, says, " It is the fruitful parent of crimes. It reverses, with respect to its object, all the rules of morality. It is nothing less than a temporary repeal of all the principles of virtue. It is a system out of which almost all the virtues are excluded; and in which nearly all the vices are incorporated." Now if a Court of Nations should prevent but one war in a whole century, all the trouble and expense of organizing such a Court would be amply repaid.

*CHAPTER XIII.

MEANS TO BE USED FOR THE PURPOSE OF OBTAINING A CON-
GRESS OF NATIONS.

1. The same means as are used in other moral enterprises—2. Miseries, crimes,
and sins of war exposed—3. Enlighten the people.

1. THE means of hastening " a consummation so devoutly
to be wished," as the organization of a Congress and Court
of Nations, are much the same as those which have been used,
to further other benevolent operations of the day. When
Sharpe, Wilberforce and Clarkson attempted the great
reformation which they so successfully accomplished, they
began with exposing the horrors and crimes of the slave
trade. Persons were employed to collect facts, and lay
them before the public in popular lectures. The press was
engaged in showing the cruelty and injustice of the traffic,
by tracts and newspaper essays; and the pulpit thundered
its anathemas against it. By the united attacks of this triple
alliance, the strongholds of the slave trade were demolished;
and nations which had before sanctioned it, now pronounced
it piracy.

2. Let the same be done in the cause of Peace. Let the
miseries, the crimes, the sins of war be detected, and vividly
portrayed before the power that rules the nation. In
* 120 republican governments and * limited monarchies, this
power lies in the people. It is vain to expect, that
governments will be moved, until the people are — for, in
representative governments, all reforms must necessarily
commence with the people. In countries where the power

lies in a monarch, he must be addressed, on the subject; for, in such governments, it is the monarch who chiefly gives the tone to public opinion, though he himself is often under its influence. All monarchs love to be popular at home and abroad. Like other men, they love praise, or glory, as they call it, and will fight for it, so long as fighting insures them the applause of the world. The same men would pursue a pacific policy, if it were more popular; and we have reason to hope, that there are even some who would do so, if it were not popular. Henry IV, though a monarch almost absolute, devised a plan, the professed object of which was nearly the same as ours, though the means of its accomplishment, and the manner in which it was to be conducted, were very different from ours. He was seconded by Elizabeth, queen of England, whose power was limited by a parliament, of which a part was elected by the people and a part was an hereditary aristocracy; and by Switzerland and other confederated republics. The form of government was no obstacle to the " great proposal," nor would it be to our Congress of Nations.

3. Though we indulge high expectations from such monarchs as the present king of Prussia, who has shown himself to be, in many things, far in advance of the spirit of * 121 the age, yet our hope relies * chiefly on the United States, Great Britain, and France, pretty much in proportion to the voice which the people have in the government. The first step, then, is to enlighten the *people,* as has been done in the State of Massachusetts; and they will call on their State Legislatures with success, as they have done in that State, and as they have done in Maine and Vermont, but the people being less enlightened on the subject, in these two States, the cause has not yet met with similar success there. The people need more light. When a

majority of the State Legislatures shall call on the general government, in as decided a tone as Massachusetts has done, Congress will fall in with the plan, for it will be popular. Our government will then call on the government of Great Britain, where light has been spreading; and the British government will yield to the solicitation of its own subjects, and our Executive; and both together will call on France. If no more than these three powers are gained, the cause is ours; and the Congress of Nations may go into immediate operation; and when the delegates of these three powers are assembled, they may extend their invitation to the other powers of Christendom. Switzerland, where much has already been done on the subject, would soon join, and the South American republics, as soon as they have consolidated their governments. The confederations of Germany, with Belgium, Holland, Denmark, and Sweden, would not be backward, as soon as they saw that the plan was likely to succeed. The philanthropic and enlightened king of *122 Prussia * would not be far behind them; and Russia and Austria would not see such great movements going on, without taking a part; but they would go on, whether these powers took a part in them or not. Spain, Portugal, and Italy would come at last; and it would be no wonder, if this generation should not pass away before the Grand Sultan and the Bey of Egypt will submit their disputes to a Court of Nations. The storm of war would soon be hushed in Christendom, and that main obstacle to the conversion of the heathen being removed, Christianity would soon spread all over the world.

*CHAPTER XIV.

ON THE DUTY OF ALL MEN, BOTH RULERS AND SUBJECTS, TO ENDEAVOR TO OBTAIN A CONGRESS OF NATIONS.

1. Nations have no moral right to declare war, until they have exhausted all the means of preserving peace—2. The physical evils of war should be prevented—3. Also the moral evils—4. Neglect of duty.

1. IT is a generally acknowledged principle, that nations have no moral right to go to war, until they have tried to preserve peace by every lawful and honorable means. This, the strongest advocate for war, in these enlightened days, will not deny, whatever might have been the opinion of mankind, on the subject, in darker ages. When a nation has received an injury, if it be of such a magnitude as, in the opinion of the injured party, ought not to be submitted to; the first thing to be done is to seek an explanation from the injuring nation; and it will be often found, that the injury was unintentional, or that it originated in misapprehension and mistake, or that there is no real ground of offence. Even where the ground of offence is undeniable, and, in the opinion of the world, the injured nation has a *right* to declare war, it is now generally believed, that they are not so likely to obtain redress and reparation by war as by forbearance and negotiation; and that it is their * 124 bounden * duty, both to themselves and to the world at large, to exhaust every means of negotiation, before they plunge themselves and other nations into the horrors and crimes of war. The United States had much ground of complaint against Great Britain, during Washington's

administration. Instead of declaring war, Jay was sent to England, and full and complete satisfaction was obtained for all the injuries received, by the influence of moral power alone, for we had not then a single ship of war on the ocean. At a subsequent period, with twice the population, and twenty times the means of offence, impatient of a protracted negotiation, we resorted to war, and got no reparation of injuries, or satisfaction whatever, except revenge, bought at an enormous expense of men and money, and made peace, leaving every cause of complaint in the *statu quo ante bellum*. Had we protracted the negotiation thirty days longer, the war and all its evils, physical and moral, would have been avoided. Sometimes negotiations have failed altogether to obtain redress. Then an offer of arbitration should follow. Now what we are seeking for is, a regular system of arbitration, and the organization of a board of arbitrators, composed of the most able civilians in the world, acting on well-known principles, established and promulgated by a Congress of Nations. If there were such a Court, no civilized nation could refuse to leave a subject of international dispute to its adjudication. Nations have tried war long enough. It has never settled any principle, and * 125 generally leaves * dissensions worse than it found them. It is, therefore, high time for the Christian world to seek a more rational, cheap, and equitable mode of settling international difficulties.

2. When we consider the horrible calamities which war has caused, the millions of lives it has cost, and the unutterable anguish which it produces, not only on the battlefield and in the military hospital, but in the social circle and the retired closet of the widow and orphan, we have reason to conclude, that the inquisition, the slave trade, slavery, and intemperance, all put together, have not caused half

so much grief and anguish to mankind as war. It is the duty, therefore, of every *philanthropist,* and every *statesman,* to do what they can to support a measure which will probably prevent many a bloody war, even if the probability were but a faint one.

3. When we consider that war is the hotbed of every crime, and that it is the principal obstacle to the conversion of the heathen, and that it sends millions unprepared suddenly into eternity, every *Christian* ought to do all he can to prevent the evil in every way in his power, not only by declaiming against war, and showing its sin and folly, but by assisting to bring forward a plan which is calculated to lessen the horrors and frequency of war. Should all the endeavors of every philanthropist, statesman and Christian in the world be successful in preventing only one war, it would be a rich reward for their labor. If only once in * 126 a century, two nations should * be persuaded to leave their disputes to a Court of Nations, and thereby one war be avoided, all the expense of maintaining such a court would be repaid with interest.

4. We therefore conclude, that every man, whether his station be public or private, who refuses to lend his aid in bringing forward this plan of a Congress and Court of Nations, neglects his duty to his country, to the world, and to God, and does not act consistently with the character of a statesman, philanthropist, or Christian.

*CHAPTER XV.

RECAPITULATION AND CONCLUSION.

I FIND I have, without any previous design, divided my
subject into the four following distinct parts:

I. 1st. I have shown what our object is. In this I have
differed from the preceding authors, and, also, from my own
previous writings on this subject, by dividing it into two
distinct branches, viz., 1st. A Congress of Nations for the
establishment of a *code of international laws* and other
purposes promoting the peace and happiness of mankind;
and, 2d, a Court of Nations entirely distinct from the Congress, though organized by it, for the purpose of *arbitrating*
or *adjudicating* all disputes referred to it by the mutual
consent of two or more contending nations. The first I
would call the legislative, the second the judiciary power,
entirely distinct from it — the first periodical, the other
perpetual. For the executive we trust to public
* 128 opinion. 2d. I have treated of the * organization of
the Congress of Nations, composed of delegates from
such powers as should choose to be represented there, each
delegation to be as numerous as the nation sending it should
choose, but entitled to only one voice or vote; and the recep-

tion of new members is provided for. 3d. I have mentioned some of the subjects to be discussed, such as the rights of belligerents toward each other, and the possibility of lessening the physical evils of war. 4th. I have treated of the rights of belligerents toward neutrals, which should be clearly defined; and, 5th, the rights of neutrals established and enlarged. 6th. I have also touched on some principles of a civil nature, which might be settled by this Congress of Nations.

II. 1st. I have, secondly, given my views of a Court of Nations organized by the Congress, for the peaceful adjudication of such international disputes as should be referred to it by the mutual consent of any two or more contending nations; and, 2d, I have given some examples, taken from both ancient and modern history, of institutions somewhat similar to a Congress and Court of Nations, among which, I dwelt particularly on the Congress of Panama, and showed the reasons of its failure — reasons not likely to occur again; and, 3d, I have given an account of some of the attempts of private individuals and peace societies to call the attention of mankind to this subject.

III. 1st. I have also stated the common objections which are raised against a Congress or Court of Nations, and * 129 have endeavored to answer them; and * have, 2d, stated some of the reasons which we have to hope that this plan will, at no distant day, be carried into effect; and, 3d, have endeavored to show a few of the benefits which would accrue from it. 4th. I have shown the means by which this great work may be accomplished; and, 5th, produced a few of the arguments, to show that it is the duty of every man to do all he can, to assist in bringing it forward.

IV. In conclusion, I would only remark, that if we have

done no other good, by procuring and publishing these Essays, we have set up a landmark, for the guidance of those who may succeed us. When the American Peace Society first entered on this work, there were only two Essays in the whole world on the subject, viz., Penn's and St. Pierre's, both very meagre, crude and undigested. Beside these, we had only what could be gathered from Sully's account of the Great Scheme of Henry IV. Now within these ten years, there have been about fifty dissertations written, many lectures delivered, and petitions presented to State legislatures, and resolutions, favorable to the plan, passed. Petitions have also been presented to the American congress, with a report on them widely circulated, and a petition to the British parliament; and the subject has been much discussed, both in public and private, and there has been evidently a great advance in public opinion, in favor of the plan, which needs only to be fully and extensively understood to insure

its adoption by all the enlightened nations of Chris-
* 130 tendom; which adoption will insure * the extension
of Christendom to the earth's remotest bounds. Finally, to adopt the language of St. Pierre, at the close of his Dissertation, " We cannot, indeed, take upon us to say that the sovereigns of Europe [and the republics of America] will actually adopt our plan, but we can safely say, that they would adopt it, if they only knew their own true interests; for it should be observed, that we have not supposed men to be such as they ought to be, good, generous, and disinterested, and public spirited, from motives of humanity; but, on the contrary, such as they really are, unjust, avaricious, and more solicitous for their private interest, than for the public good. The only supposition which we have made is, that mankind have sense enough, in general, to know what is useful to them, and fortitude enough

to embrace the means of their own happiness. Should our plan, nevertheless, fail of being put into execution, it will not be because it is chimerical, but because the world is absurd; and there is a kind of absurdity in being wise among fools."

APPENDIX.

No. 1.

Extracts from the " Speech of Don Manuel Lorenzo Vidaurre, Minister from Peru, at the opening of the American Congress of Panama, on the 22d of June, 1826."

THIS day, the great American Congress, which is to be a council in the hour of conflict, the faithful interpreter of treaties, a mediator in domestic contentions, and which is charged with the formation of our new body of international law, has been organized and invested with all the powers competent to attain the important and dignified end for which it is convoked. All the precious materials are prepared to our hand. A world regards our labors with the deepest attention. From the most powerful monarch, to the humblest peasant of the Southern continent, no one views our task with indifference. This will be the last opportunity for the attempt to prove that man can be happy. Let us, then, proudly stand forth the representatives of millions of freemen, and, inspired with a noble complacency, assimilate ourselves to the Creator himself, when he first gave laws to the universe.

Animated with celestial fire, and looking steadily and with reverence to the Author of our being, *difficulties the most appalling shrink into insignificance.* The basis of our confederation is firm: *Peace with the whole world;* respect for European governments, even where their political principles are diametrically opposed to those acknowledged in America; *free commerce* with all nations, and a diminution of imposts on the trade of such as have acknowledged our independence; *religious toleration* for such as observe different rites from those
* 132   established by * our constitution. How emphatically are we taught by the
blood which fanaticism has spilt, from the time of the Jews to the commencement of the present century, to be compassionate and tolerant to all who travel to the same point by different paths. Let the stranger, of whatever mode or faith, come hither; he shall be protected and respected, unless his morals, the true standard of religion, be opposed to the system given us by the Messiah. Let him come and instruct us in agriculture and the arts. Let the sad and abject countenance of the poor African, bending under the chains of rapacity and oppression, no longer be seen in these climes; let him be endowed with equal privileges with the white man, whose color he has been taught to regard as a badge of superiority; let him,

111

in learning that he is not distinct from other men, learn to become a rational being.

As respects ourselves, two dangers are principally to be avoided. The desire of aggrandizement in one state at the expense of another, and the possibility that some ambitious individual will aspire to enslave and tyrannize over his fellow-citizens. Both of these are as much to be apprehended, as the weak efforts of the Spaniards are to be contemned. Human passions will always operate, and can never be extinguished; nor, indeed, should we wish to stifle them. Man is always aspiring, and never content with present possessions; he has always been iniquitous, and can we at once inspire him with a love of justice? *I trust we can.* He has had a dire experience of the ravages which uncontrolled passion has caused.

Sully and Henry IV projected a tribunal which should save Europe from the first of these calamities. In our own day, Gordon has written a treatise on the same subject. This assembly realizes the laudable views of the king and the philosopher. *Let us avoid war, by a common and uniform reference to negotiation.*

Above all, let us form one family, and forget the names of our respective countries in the more general denomination of brothers; let us trade without restrictions,—without prohibition,—let articles of American growth be free from duty in all our ports—let us give each other continual proofs of confidence, disinterestedness and true friendship; let us form a body of public law, which the civilized world may admire; in it, a wrong to one state shall be regarded as an injury to all, as in a well-regulated community, injustice to an individual concerns the rest of the republic. Let us solve the problem as to the best of governments. The form which we adopt, securing to individuals all possible benefit, and to the nation the greatest advantages, is that which, beyond doubt, reaches the greatest felicity of which human nature is susceptible, the highest perfection of human institutions.

*133   *And when our labors are concluded, let us return to our homes, and, surrounded by our children and grandchildren, let us select the youngest of those beloved objects, and uplifting it, a fit offering to the Supreme Being, teach it in tender accents to give thanks for the inestimable benefits we have received. Let the Greek celebrate his exploits in leaving Troy in ashes; the representative of the American Republics will boast of having promulgated laws, which secure peace abroad as well as the internal tranquillity of the states that now confederate.

No. 2.

First Petition to the Legislature of Massachusetts.

The following Petition was presented to the Senate of Massachusetts, by the Hon. Sidney Willard, February 6, 1835:

To the Senate and House of Representatives of the Commonwealth of Massachusetts, in General Court convened, on the first Wednesday of January, A. D., 1835.

The Petition of the subscribers humbly shows: that, a proposition having been laid before a very large and respectable portion of the community, in relation to a reference by the Peace Societies to the attention of Congress on the subject of an Abolition of War, by devising suitable means for the references of all international disputes to a Court of Nations, to be established either permanently or otherwise, in such form and manner as the best counsel and wisdom of the several nations may hereafter deem proper to adopt; which proposition, it appears, had received the countenance, and the signatures in its favor, of several thousand individuals, in this and other States, among whom are many of our fellow-citizens of eminent rank, talent, and character, those also of all classes and professions in the community, of all political parties, and of every religious denomination: the subscribers, deeply impressed with a consideration of the burdensome expense, the moral corruption, the manifold crimes, the private suffering, and the public calamities incurred by war; considering it inconsistent with the spirit of Christianity, injurious to the physical, moral, social, and religious condition of the community, productive of immense evils, and subversive, in many respects, of the best interests of mankind; lamenting the insensibility which habit and education have induced with respect to this custom; believing the decision of international disputes on principles of equity, without an ap-
* 134 peal to arms, to be * dictated by enlightened reason, demanded by Christian duty, commended by every consideration of self-interest, and, therefore, loudly called for by the voice of wisdom; and seeing the steps now taking by eminent philanthropists, statesmen, and others, in Great Britain, and on the continent of Europe, to cooperate with the citizens of the United States, in relation to such measures as may be deemed expedient and practicable, to procure its abolition; wishing to awaken, yet more widely and effectually, the attention of the public to its baneful influence on the agricultural, the commercial, and the manufacturing interests, and on the progress of civilization, arts, sciences, and religion; desirous of investigating the means best adapted for the promotion of permanent and universal peace, and of establishing the conviction that the highest dignity of a people results from the exercise of impartial justice towards all nations, and that the highest happiness of a community can be attained only by cherishing the spirit and virtues of peace; in a word, considering it of the utmost importance to the best interests of humanity, civilization, and improvement, that some mode of just arbitration should be established for the amicable and final adjustment of all international disputes, instead of an appeal to arms, request the attention of your honorable body to this, as we deem, highly important subject, in order that such steps may be taken in relation thereto, as may appear best adapted to promote the end in view.

THOMAS THOMPSON, JR.,
WM. LADD, *Gen. Agent of A. P. S.*

No. 3.

Report on the foregoing Petition.

Commonwealth of Massachusetts.

The Committee of the Senate, to whom was referred the Petition of Thomas Thompson, Jr., and Wm. Ladd, General Agent of the American Peace Society, REPORT:

That they have considered said petition, which sets forth that several thousand persons in this Commonwealth and other States, have signed a proposition calling on the peace societies, at a suitable time, to present petitions to Congress, praying that measures may be taken, in connection with other governments, to refer all international disputes to a Court of Nations, with a view to prevent a * 135 resort to war, for the * obtaining of alleged rights, or the reparation of injuries. The petitioners enumerate several of the prominent evils of war, evils which can hardly be exaggerated, and request the attention of the General Court to the subject, "in order that such steps may be taken in relation thereto as may appear best adapted to promote the end in view."

The Committee, during the interval which has elapsed since the petition was referred to them, have taken a deep interest in the subject of it; but they have felt embarrassed by that diffidence which lays its restraints upon all men who are not marked out by their constitutional temperament for reformers, and who are placed in such a novel situation, when,—from the humble beginnings of small associations, scattered in different territories of the civilized parts of the earth, toiling and praying for the peace of nations,—they have looked forward to the glorious consummation devoutly wished, and confidently expected, at some period of the world's eventful history.

The Committee are fully persuaded that pacific principles are gaining ground. Mankind are more and more convinced, that wars are generally waged, not only without necessity, but even in defiance of wisdom and humanity. They are more and more inclined to believe that something founded in the pride, or ambition, or deep-laid policy of rulers, is commonly the great stake, rather than the interests of their subjects. And finding that the objects held out as pretexts for hostilities are rarely, if ever, accomplished, or, if gained, at a sacrifice with which the amount of the benefit sinks to nothing in comparison; just views of the interests of man are leading the more intelligent to count the cost of these great games of princes and statesmen, which are played at infinite expense,—expense not only of individual and national wealth, but of domestic happiness and of public morals,—and above all, expense of human life, the value of which is not a subject for computation.

It is thought by the Committee, that the appointment of some umpire, either temporary or permanent, by which disputes between nations may be decided, is by no means a visionary project. Such an umpire can certainly be designated, whenever public opinion, in civilized nations, shall be sufficiently enlightened to sanction it. It is already embraced in the views of our extending peace societies, in the discussions and lectures of our lyceums, in the debates of our academic halls; and it is believed that the Legislature of this Commonwealth would not go far in advance of public opinion, by some declarative act favorable to this pacific mode of terminating the controversies of nations. Such a declaration would at least be harmless; and no man of high moral feeling or moral courage can hesitate how to act, when the alternative presented is, on the one * 136 hand, the possibility of accomplishing an * incalculable public good, and on the other, nothing but the danger of encountering the chilling incredulity or heartless raillery of those who do not know how to appreciate his motives.

If we may reason from the less to the greater, from plans well known, and already tried with success, to those which have not been attempted on a more comprehensive system, and which may prove more complex in their operations, such an umpire as has been suggested is not impracticable. It is no novelty in a limited sphere. It is as old as the Amphictyonic Council, which came, in its progress, to embrace deputies from thirty-one cities or states; a council whose decisions upon the disputes between the cities of Greece were for a time sacredly and inviolably regarded. And, in modern times, the Swiss cantons, with their variety of nations and languages, of manners, of religion, especially of the two great antagonist divisions, Catholic and Protestant, and of governments, too, from unmixed democracy to stern aristocracy, have, by their Diet, or Court of Ambassadors, preserved among the members of the confederacy that uniform peace and resistance to foreign aggression, for which the union of those two and twenty independent states was formed.

If a public attempt is ever to be made to bring war into discredit, and to devise some amicable mode of settling disputes between nations, it may be well now for some public body to feel the way. And no where can this beginning be more suitable than in Massachusetts. It is in this Commonwealth, if we except the Friends or Quakers, that the earliest and most unintermitted efforts have been made to diffuse the principles of universal peace. The Massachusetts Peace Society is looking to us for encouragement. The trustees, in their recent report, after alluding to the motion made last year in the Legislature, recommending a Court of Nations for the securing permanent peace, add, "Should the measure be renewed at the present session, and meet with success, we shall hail it as a most felicitous and honorable event." It is a small boon that they ask at our hands. They assume the labor; they entreat from us, who cannot but have the same noble purpose at heart, to speak an approving word. They will be satisfied with a simple declaration, such as the Committee are about to propose; such, as it is presumed, will not be withheld.

If we are asked what effects are to flow from this measure, we answer, It will show the people of this Commonwealth, that when solicited to express an opinion upon a great national subject of vital concern, a subject which can excite no conflict of party passions, we do not turn a deaf ear to the call; that we do not maintain a heartless silence, but return a kind and generous

* 137 response to the voice of those * noble philanthropists who would save mankind from evils, into which those in times gone by have rushed headlong, and which they have been obliged to rue when it was too late to escape them.

We may hope that an example so inoffensive, so reasonable, so well intended, aiming at the highest interests of humanity, "Peace on earth and good-will to men," will not be overlooked; that it will be followed by other States, and when, in this way, a wider influence shall be produced upon public opinion, may it not be hoped that the object will be recommended with such power to the general government, as to lead to salutary action, resulting through its negotiations with other powers, in more benevolent and well-defined principles of international law, tending to cut off many of the occasions of national conflicts, and, if not to put a final period to wars, at least to disarm them of some of their horrors? With this brief and very imperfect view of the subject, the Committee unanimously recommend the following resolutions for the adoption of the Legislature.

SIDNEY WILLARD,
DANIEL MESSINGER, } Committee.
EPHRAIM HASTINGS,

Commonwealth of Massachusetts.

In the year of our Lord one thousand eight hundred and thirty-five.

Resolved, That in the opinion of this Legislature, some mode should be established for the amicable and final adjustment of all international disputes, instead of resort to war.

Resolved, That the Governor of this Commonwealth be requested to communicate a copy of the above report and of the resolutions annexed, to the Executive of each of the States, to be laid before the Legislature thereof, inviting a cooperation for the advancement of the object in view.

No. 4.

To the Honorable Senate and House of Representatives of the Commonwealth of Massachusetts in General Court convened on the first Wednesday of January, A. D., 1837.

The memorial of the undersigned humbly shows,—That a proposition having been by him, sometime since, suggested in favor of calling the attention of * 138 Congress or inviting that of the head of the Executive * Government of the Union, in concert with such other governments as may see fit to unite in counsel with the United States, for the establishment of a Congress or Court of Nations, either permanent or otherwise, in such form and manner as the best counsel and wisdom of the several nations may deem proper to adopt, or for considering such measures as may be deemed most suitable for devising, if possible, and introducing as far as may be practicable, some other system of arbitration for the settlement of international disputes, which shall be more congenial with the intellectual, moral, and religious, as well as the physical advancement of the age, than an appeal to arms, a custom now beginning to be very generally considered by the enlightened of all civilized, and more especially all Christian communities, as a relic of barbarism, and as always uncertain and wholly inadequate to the speedy, just, and full redress of grievances; which proposition has received the countenance and the signatures, in its favor, of a great number of individuals eminent in rank, talent, and character, both in this and other States, and also those of all classes and professions, of different political parties, and of every religious denomination: believing a state of society has developed itself in the United States, and also in some of the more enlightened and republican nations of Europe, of the existence of which the governments of the respective countries have not, by any acts in conformity thereto, appeared to be aware, and for which no adequate preparation, nor any appropriate change in the existing state of things has yet been made; a state of society by which, it appears to your memorialist, the present age is strongly marked, and whose features distinguish it most clearly and prominently from all preceding times; a state of society in which national wealth is no longer obtained by conquest, the precarious acquisition of some bold, restless and ambitious military chieftain, but by the private, individual exertion of the intelligence, industry and activity of the citizens at large, in the pursuit of their several peaceful professions and occupations; a state of society which, differing so widely and so totally in all its ways and all its wants from that preceding it, cannot be adequately fostered, provided for and protected by those institutions and laws which were instituted and enacted for the regulation, government, and well-being of communities, so widely differing in circumstances and resources, where might constitutes the only effective right, where stealth was countenanced by law, when the sword occupied the place of the batoon, and the strong arm was the only avenger: seeing in the present state of things a change so marked, and indeed so radical and apparently so permanent a revolution, requiring at least some modification of those rules and regulations which were enacted with * 139 not the * most remote anticipation of the now existing actual condition of a very large and continually increasing portion of society, a community embracing the farmer, the manufacturer, the merchant, the mechanic, the trader, not to name more particularly the various liberal professions and many other minor classes of citizens, all peacefully, privately, actively, and usefully engaged in those various individual employments which tend so directly and so effectually to promote, establish and extend that highly cultivated and refined state of civilization, so powerfully promotive of the useful arts and sciences and all the higher interests of man, and whose development can only be effectually attained where man is in the enjoyment of perfect freedom, equal rights, and peace: considering the many deep-rooted, and wide-spread evils of war, its invariably adverse bearing on the best interests of mankind, undermining the physical, moral, social and religious condition of the community, imposing the most burdensome expense, introducing the darkest crimes, extending the deepest corruption, creating the keenest individual suffering, social miseries, and public calamities: perceiving the growing disinclination to all acts of brutal violence, the enlightened opposition already made by associated individuals, incorporated public bodies, and various legislative and executive authorities, not only in the United States but also in many parts of Europe, to the outbreaking of popular violence, the sanguinary indulgence of private passion, and even the inexpedient secret arming of individuals for the real or declared purpose of self-defence, and remarking, also, the highly honorable attitude assumed by the public press in various parts of this and other countries in favor of peace: regretting, and desirous, if possible, to remove, the widely prevailing insensibility to the futility, inexpediency, and folly of war, an insensibility induced only by the combined effect of erroneous principles of instruction, long prevalent custom and utter want of due reflection: believing the introduction of some system for the equitable settlement of international disputes, without an appeal to arms, when once sanctioned by the popular favor, to be perfectly practicable, as much so as any at present in existence, for the legal decision of disputes between individuals, incorporated bodies, towns, districts and states; and, being thus practicable, to be demanded by the voice of common humanity, by the dictates of enlightened reason, by the obligations of Christian duty, by the prompting of self-interest and by considerations of public good: being informed of the inclination and exertions of many distinguished philanthropists, scholars, statesmen and others in Great Britain and on the continent of Europe, to cooperate with the friends of peace in the United States for the adoption of such measures * 140 as may appear to be most expedient and * practicable for the introduction of some system of arbitration instead of an appeal to arms: desirous of calling the attention of the public, and of our several state and general governments, more immediately and effectually to this subject, in order, from a consideration of the baneful influence of war on the agricultural, commercial, manufacturing and various mechanic interests, on the progress of civilization, arts, sciences and religion, the extensive acquisition of national wealth, and the secure enjoyment of the fruits of private industry, to extend and strengthen a conviction, that the highest dignity of a people results from the exercise of impartial justice towards all nations; and the highest happiness of a community can be attained only by cherishing the spirit and virtues of peace: thus proving it to be of the utmost importance to the best interests of civilization, freedom, human improvement, and the refinements of social life, to establish some mode of just arbitration, for the amicable and final adjustment of all international disputes, instead of an appeal to arms: Your memorialist requests the attention of your honorable body to this, as he deems it, and as he has reason to believe, the great body of the people, not only of this State and the other members of our confederacy, but those of other countries, also, think it to be, highly important subject, in order that such steps may be taken in relation thereto as may appear to be best adapted to promote the end in view.

THOMAS THOMPSON, JR.

House of Representatives, Feb. 18, 1837.—Referred to the special committee on the subject thereof sent up for concurrence.

L. S. CUSHING, *Clerk.*

Senate, Feb. 20, 1837.—Concurred.

CHARLES CALHOUN, *Clerk.*

No. 5.

Petition of the Executive Committee of the Massachusetts Peace Society.

To the Honorable Senate and House of Representatives of the Commonwealth of Massachusetts in General Court assembled:—The memorial of the undersigned, members of the Executive Committee of the Massachusetts Peace Society, respectfully shows:

That the Society which we represent has existed for upwards of twenty * 141 years, and has comprised a considerable number of the citizens * of this Commonwealth, some of whom have been distinguished for elevated stations in the community, for talent, benevolence and respectability of character, who have associated themselves together with the design of abolishing, by moral means, one of the greatest evils of the human race—the practice of national war. They have been encouraged in the promotion of this design, by the full belief that war does not occur from any natural, or irresistible necessity, but entirely from the excited passions, mistaken interests, and deep delusions of nations, and may therefore be prevented by moral influence and exposition judiciously applied so as to enlighten the reason and consciences of men. In these sentiments, and corresponding conduct, they have received the full concurrence of other similar institutions in the United States and foreign countries.

Among the various measures which have been proposed for checking the spirit and practice of war, a prominent place has been given to the idea of an international Congress or Court, composed of delegates from all the civilized foreign powers, which should consider and determine the disputed questions arising between them, in cases which have hitherto been supposed to require an appeal to arms, and the award of which should be considered as binding, in honor, on the disputing parties. This project has occupied the attention of our Society for a long time, and a proposition, comprising it, has been extensively presented to individuals of all ranks and classes in this State, by whom it has been almost unanimously and readily accepted. It was our intention to have submitted this proposition, and our views upon it, to the government of the United States, but having recently learned, that your honorable bodies have referred this subject to a joint committee, we have thought that an expression of the associated friends of peace was peculiarly proper, while it was thus under consideration. A meeting of the Massachusetts Peace Society has accordingly been held, and we, their

Executive Committee, have been directed, in their name, and on their behalf, to offer to you their views and desires on this subject.

In the execution of this trust, your memorialists deem it unnecessary to lay before you any demonstration of the immorality and the misery of war, to which all history bears ample testimony, and of which you doubtless are fully aware, and we feel confident we shall address none, who do not sincerely desire its extinction. It is only incumbent on us, to present to you the views of our Society on the practicability and efficacy of the measure now proposed for that purpose. We are enjoined to request of your honorable houses, that if it seems meet to you, some expression of opinion may be made by you, which may * 142 be * communicated to the President of the United States conveying the desire that he would open a negotiation with other foreign powers, for the purpose of establishing, by their general consent, some such impartial tribunal, for the adjustment of international differences, as we have suggested.

On the practicability of such an arrangement, your memorialists would remark, that it has been fully discussed in the assemblies and publications of the friends of peace, and has been very generally determined in the affirmative, by all who have treated it, including many minds by no means disposed to be sanguine or visionary. To this we may add, that rational governments have also indicated their approbation of the principle of this course, by submission of disputes to other governments as impartial arbiters—a measure to which our own government has more than once resorted.

It may be objected to the object of our solicitation, that it would not be proper for the legislature of this or any other State to make any recommendation on a subject of foreign polity, which is considered as belonging exclusively to the government of the United States. On this point, your own wisdom will decide, and it does not become us to offer any opinion; we may, however, be pardoned for the remark, that we cannot think such an application, coming in a spirit of philanthropy from so respected and influential a member of the Union, would be regarded as improper interference with the prerogatives of the general government; nor should we consider the negotiation which it proposes hopeless of a favorable result, in the present political state of the world, proceeding from a nation whose form of government and remoteness from the collisions of other great powers would preclude all suspicion of sinister motives.

To this—our beloved country—we earnestly desire the honor of offering to the world this truly rational policy, which a more enlightened posterity will elevate far above the renown of violent revolutions and extensive conquests, and to our own Commonwealth, to which has been awarded the merited reputation of advance in many works of Christian benevolence, we would hope to add the imperishable glory of first pointing out the merciful refuge of peace.

Respectfully submitted by direction of the Massachusetts Peace Society.

CHARLES LOWELL,	THOS. VOSE,
ROBERT WATERSTON,	J. P. BLANCHARD,
BARON STOW,	WM. BRIGHAM,
J. V. HIMES,	BRADFORD SUMNER.

No. 6.

* 143   *Report on the foregoing Petitions.*

Commonwealth of Massachusetts.

IN SENATE, April 4, 1837.

The Joint Special Committee, to whom was referred an Order of the 15th ultimo, for the consideration of the expediency of memorializing Congress, or the Executive of the United States, on the subject of opening a negotiation with such other governments as may be deemed most judicious, with a view of establishing a Congress or Court of Nations, to be either permanent or otherwise, for considering such measures as may be deemed most suitable for devising and introducing some other system, more congenial with the moral and religious, as well as physical advancement of the age, than an appeal to arms, for a redress of national grievances; and to whom, also, was referred the Memorials of Thomas Thompson, Jr. and the Executive Committee of the Massachusetts Peace Society, in reference to this subject, REPORT:

That they have had the subject under consideration; and, after giving it that attention its merits appear to deserve, have become deeply impressed with a full conviction of the highly beneficial results which may be attained by the prosecution of such measures as are now in contemplation; and freely express their impression, that the proposition, set forth in the order and memorials referred to the Committee, is neither visionary in theory, unimportant in character, nor unattainable in result; but, on the contrary, appears to this Committee to be well deserving the countenance and cordial support of every friend to the stability of the social compact, the increase of national wealth, the advancement of civilization, the promotion of the arts and sciences, the extension of freedom, the security of constitutional government, the improvement of public morals, the extension of the Christian faith, and thus to the general welfare of mankind.

In arriving at this result, your Committee have gone over a wide field of observation and inquiry.

The proposition now under consideration, however novel it may appear to many, has been, for six years past, a subject of interest, attention and discussion in this community.

It appears, from well authenticated facts, and many printed and written documents, presented by the memorialists to the Committee, that there has
* 144 been a very wide and full expression of sentiment from * all classes of the community, without distinction of party, sect or profession, in favor of the measures now in contemplation in reference to a Congress or Court of Nations, for the amicable adjustment of international disputes. Among those who have given their signatures in favor of the proposition, your Committee find the names of a great number of individuals of the highest rank in regard to social,

intellectual, moral, political, and religious attainment. Among them are some of those who have filled the highest executive and judicial offices of this Commonwealth and of other States, many of the most eminent of our counsellors and statesmen; and the clergy, the most intelligent merchants, manufacturers, mechanics, and farmers, also masters of vessels appear to have come forward in bodies to enrol their names in favor of this cause. In our colleges, academies, and public and private schools, its reception appears to have been equally favorable; presidents, professors, tutors, instructers, and the students of the higher classes uniting in its support; in furtherance of which, it appears, peace societies have recently been formed by the associated instructers and students at many of our colleges and literary institutions; and orations and other exercises on this topic have been assigned at commencement and on other occasions; and, in some cases, prizes are statedly assigned and medals are awarded for the best dissertations and poems on the subject of peace, and of arbitration as a substitute for an appeal to arms. Very many and strongly expressed resolves have been passed with perfect unanimity in a number of ecclesiastical and lay conventions, associations, conferences, and other meetings. Indeed, so very favorably has this cause been received by the community at large, it appears that there are about a thousand clergymen in the New England, Middle, Western and Southern States, who have given their names pledging themselves to preach at least one sermon every year on this subject; and it is introduced in lyceum lectures and discussions, and made an object of attention in Bible classes, and in the course of instruction in Sabbath schools. Many of the most popular and talented authors have proffered their services in the promotion of this cause; and Sabbath school books, and books for other schools and academies, and some works of a still higher class, having reference to its promotion, have been published, as is shown by the memorialists, not only in several of the New England States, but also at the South, in London, Switzerland, and elsewhere. It appears, further, from facts and documents presented to your Committee by the memorialists, an extensive correspondence on this subject has been carried on, for some time past, between societies and individuals in various parts of the United States, Great *145 Britain, France, Switzerland, *Prussia, Holland, some of the German States, and elsewhere; meetings have been held, societies formed, addresses made, and resolves adopted; from which there appears to be a very wide spread and prevailing sentiment in favor of a general cooperation for the attainment of the great and all-important design of substituting arbitration instead of arms, as a last resort, for the decision of international disputes. Several of the courts of Europe have been addressed on the subject of peace by the Count de Sellon.

Your Committee have deemed it proper, and, indeed, in a degree, essential, to the interests of this cause, to give the foregoing very brief outline of the facts laid before them, in regard to the state of feeling apparently prevailing in the community, both in this country and abroad, in favor of some action, on the part of government, for the promotion of the object now presented to view. It cannot be denied, the view opens a bright field of intelligence and high moral feeling, unfolding a wide expanse of heart-cheering philanthropy; a field appearing already ripe for the harvest, and open for him who will, to enter in, and be the first to win its laurels, to pluck its rich and wholesome fruit, and gather to himself a rich store of present fame, future and fair renown, and a glory which shall endure, when the blood-stained laurels of the offensive warrior shall have become faded and withered, an object of the abhorrence rather than the veneration of mankind.

May not the citizens of this State, and of these United States, be justly indulged in the laudable desire of seeing one of their own chief magistrates the first to set foot on this thrice consecrated ground? May they not pardonably indulge the flattering hope to see the name of a president of this republic engraved on that ever-enduring and consecrated list, where stand, and will for ever remain, so long as the memory of man shall endure, the names of Numa Pompilius, Francis the first, of France, Charles the fifth, of the Low Countries, Cæsar Maximilian the emperor, Henry the eighth, of England, W. A. Ciervier, John Sylvagius, chancellor of Burgundy, Erasmus, Fenelon, Henry the fourth, of France, and Charles Irene Castel de St. Pierre. If the remembrance of these names is cherished by the enlightened of the present day, with a feeling approaching to veneration, for their individual efforts in the cause of peace, with how warm and heartfelt an admiration will his name and memory be embalmed in the cherished recollection of a grateful world, whose far-sighted policy, active philanthropy, and skilful diplomacy, shall summon, not his kindred, not his fellow-townsmen, not his political partisans and abettors, not the immediate members or confederates * 146 of his own nation merely, but the great * family of nations, to meet in a friendly council—an august assembly!—to consult together for the common good, to promote the general welfare of mankind, to cause the sword to be unsheathed, the bayonet to be unfixed, and to bid the iron-tongued artillery no longer cause the nations to quake before its thunder. Not that the memorials referred to this Committee contemplate the total discharge of your navy, the entire dismantling of your forts, the immediate disbanding of your regular troops, or the disorganizing of your militia. The sword of justice must be uplifted still. The armed police of nations must remain on the alert. The court-room does not supersede the necessity of the watch-house. Yet the trial by jury has superseded, and may well supplant the trial by combat; and arbitration, or a Court of Nations, may be made the final resort, instead of an appeal to arms.

In arriving at this conclusion, your Committee are happy in finding the opinion they have been led to adopt, founded on the result of their own investigation, supported by the deliberately and publicly expressed opinions of others, for whose decision, in regard to a subject of this nature, they entertain no light regard.

At a former session of the Legislature of this State, the Committee to whom was referred a petition, from one of the abovenamed memorialists, on the subject now under the consideration of your Committee, in reporting, as they did, in favor of the prayer of the petition, and unanimously recommending certain resolutions in relation thereto, which report was accepted, and the resolutions adopted in the Senate, by a vote of nineteen to five, have expressed an opinion to which your Committee are disposed cordially to respond. They say, "It is thought by the Committee that some umpire, either temporary or permanent, by which disputes between nations may be decided, is by no means a visionary project. Such an umpire will certainly be practicable, whenever public opinion, in civilized nations, shall be sufficiently enlightened to sanction it." The Committee further remark: "It is believed that the Legislature of this Commonwealth would not go far in advance of public opinion, by some declarative act favorable to this pacific mode of terminating the controversies of nations. Such a declaration, if not utterly destitute of ground to stand upon, would be at least harmless; and no man of high moral feeling, or moral courage, can hesitate how to act, when the alternative presented is, on the one hand, the possibility of accomplishing an incalculable public good, and, on the other, the danger of encountering the chilling incredulity or heartless raillery of those who do not know how to appreciate his motives."

The Committee further say: "If a public attempt is ever to be made to * 147 bring war into discredit, and to devise * some amicable mode of settling disputes between nations, it may be well now for some public body to feel the way. And no where can this beginning be more suitable than in Massachusetts." And in speaking of the effects to flow from the measure, the Committee say: "It will show the people of this Commonwealth, that when solicited to express an opinion upon a great national subject of vital concern, a subject which can excite no conflict of party passions, we do not turn a deaf ear to the call; that we do not maintain a heartless silence, but return a kind and generous response to the voice of those noble philanthropists, who would save mankind from evils into which those in times gone by have rushed headlong, and which they have been obliged to rue when it was too late to escape them." In these sentiments, your Committee think, there is a magnanimity which will insure a ready and full response from every American breast. Such sentiments, they think, cannot be too widely disseminated.

The Committee of the Society for the Promotion of Permanent and Universal Peace, established at London, in their seventeenth annual report, speaking of the proposition now under the consideration of your Committee, say: "What is there in this proposal that does not commend itself to the good sense of every man? It is only an extension of that principle of legislation, which settles private disputes by arbitration or courts of law, instead of leaving every one to right himself, which might result in violence and murder." After speaking of the doings in this country, and in Switzerland, relative to this measure, they say: "Your Committee have watched, with a lively interest, these proceedings of their brethren and fellow-laborers in America and Geneva; their own labors have not yet been in this direction, though they have, for some time past, held themselves in readiness, at a suitable opportunity, to bring this subject more immediately under the consideration of the British public and of the government." At the eighteenth annual meeting of the London Peace Society, the subject of a Court of Nations was discussed, and the following resolution was moved and carried:

"That the continuance of peace calls for our grateful acknowledgments to Almighty God, and we sincerely hope that the experience of its advantages may induce the powers of Europe and America to endeavor to prevent the recurrence of war, by the adoption of a peaceful and rational mode of settling their differences by arbitration." This meeting, and the subject discussed at it, appears to have been noticed with commendation by the British press. As an instance of the tone assumed on the occasion, the following remarks, from the London Mercantile Journal, will not be read without interest. After speaking of * 148 the rapid progress of the principles and policy of * peace, it is remarked:

"In a mercantile point of view, this subject is very important, and every mercantile man should be a member of the Peace Society. What becomes of trade during the existence of war? Is not war a total interruption of, and a complete curse to trade? And in this country, which is a commercial country, ought above all to study the things which make for peace, as upon peace commerce depends, and upon commerce England depends. Reason and experience, and not guns and swords, are the best arbiters between man and man, and ought, indeed, to be the only arbiters between rational beings.

Physical contests are the characteristics of brutes, which we do not allow to possess reason. War has hitherto been the game at which kings and generals have played, whilst the people have found them in money wherewith to carry it on; but the people are becoming wiser, and choose rather to keep their money in their pockets. But if the principles of the Peace Society were universal, there would never need be any war, even of self-defence, because there never would be any aggression. In the beautiful imagery of eastern poetry, men would convert their swords into ploughshares. Europe has now long been at peace, and may she continue to be so! and we expect that the diffusion of knowledge will increasingly secure its unnumbered blessings to all mankind. Our national debt of eight hundred millions is a monument to the folly, false glory, mischief, and curse of war. Nations, as they become enlightened, will survey this monument, and read its inscription; and the experience on this subject, which has cost us so much, will be given to them for nothing. Such is our own deep conviction of the unnecessariness, folly, ruination and mischief of all war; and such our persuasion of the advantages, wisdom and glory of peace, that we say, 'success to the Peace Society—may all society throughout both hemispheres of this well-peopled world, become one great Peace Society;' and say amen to the malediction, 'cursed be the hand that again kindles the fires of war!'"

Your Committee have quoted these remarks thus at large, believing them to be of no light import in this connection, conveying, as we have reason to think they do, the sentiments of a great and highly respectable portion of the more intelligent classes of the British public; and for the same reason we are gratified to see the publication of the following sentiment in the Quarterly Journal of the British Peace Society: it is from a Hartford County Report. "The benevolent proposal of instituting a high court, to which may be referred for equitable and final adjustment all international disputes, deserves the serious con-

sideration of the ' powers that be,' and of every friend of peace. It is hoped, that
measures may be adopted in different countries, to call forth a public
* 149 * expression of the opinion of the people, and requests, to their respective
governments to adopt this specific measure." The measure has been approved at various public meetings in different parts of Great Britain. To select
one instance from many: at a meeting of the Newcastle auxiliary to the London
Society for the Promotion of Permanent and Universal Peace, one of the speakers
observed, "he wished the Society possessed the means of extending their
principles into other countries, and then he trusted that the system of national
arbitration would become matured and generally acted on." Sentiments of individuals and societies on the continent, in France, Geneva, and elsewhere, equally
friendly to the measure, have been laid before your Committee, but they deem
further citation on this point unnecessary.

Your Committee, consistently with what they deem their duty on an occasion
like the present, and as an organ of the highest representative body in a community so enlightened as that comprising the citizens of this Commonwealth, cannot
withhold their hearty approbation of the signal instance of triumphant benevolence recently given by his majesty William IV, in his successful proffer of
friendly mediation, during the recent misunderstanding between the governments
of the United States and France: a mediation most magnanimous in its spirit,
and most honorable to the British king, as the monarch of a powerful, highly
civilized, intelligent and Christian people: a mediation most happily and fully
successful in the attainment of the unspeakably important object in view; and
hence demanding the public and grateful acknowledgments of those who were so
greatly benefited by it. A mediation indicating, in its origin, acceptance and
results, a radical change and permanent advance in public sentiment, which cannot but be regarded as most auspicious to the dearest interests of mankind; and
also as clearly demonstrating the practicability, provided the attention of the
several nations can be called to the subject, of devising, introducing and establishing some mode of determining disputes between civilized nations other than
that of an appeal to arms. In fine, a mediation, which, when the bonds of
amity were broken, when the ultimate stand had been taken, when the doors of
reconciliation were closing, when a hostile attitude was already assumed and
forces were collecting, and arms were burnishing, and navies were manned and fit-
ting out for service, bid that phantom falsely styled national honor to disappear,
caused reason to resume her seat, allowed justice to uplift her scales, and, in so
doing, prevented an astonished universe from beholding, and disburdened the pen
of the future historian from recording, yet other bloody acts, revolting
* 150 spectacles, and dismal legends to be chronicled with * those of Ostend,
Aboukir and Alexandria, the Rhine reddened and swollen with the gory
torrents successively poured into it from Tournay, Kayserslautern, Josselies,
Cologne, Manheim, Mayence, Frankenthal and Fribourg, the slaughter of the
Burmese, the desolations of the Carnatic, the massacre at Scio, the battle of
Borodino, the passage of the Beresina, and, finally, the field of Waterloo: acts

which,—while causing blood to flow in torrents, depriving old age of its prop, and infancy of its provider, extending desolation over sea and land, and introducing wretchedness to the fireside of the hovel, paralyzing the arm of industry abroad, and agonizing the heart at home; aiming a death-blow at commerce, manufactures, and the useful arts,—would nevertheless lay claim to be deemed honorable when committed by nations though they would be universally denounced as barbarous and brutish, if done by individuals. In this view of the case, your Committee ask, foreseeing these acts and dreading these then impending evils, if joy did not thrill every American heart, on hearing the noble offer of his august majesty the king of England, to become the friendly arbiter between the governments of France and the United States? two nations whose friendly intercourse and mutual good offices had, since the very commencement of our existence as a nation, been cemented by the golden chain of commerce. A noble umpirage! which may have prevented not only the estrangement of two most friendly nations, but also the waste of millions of money and the destruction of thousands of human lives, in addition to the blow, fatal it might have been, inflicted on the advance of liberal principles and the establishment of free institutions, and setting the world one more injurious example of the baneful custom of engaging in war for the assertion of right. Your Committee feel unfeigned delight in recurring to this most magnanimous instance of enlightened policy in the government of that country in whose just fame the citizens of the United States will ever feel a pride, regarding and cherishing it in memory as the mother country, in whose bosom was fostered that attachment to liberal principles, and that love of freedom, to which this republic is indebted for its being.

Your Committee have thus laid before you the results of their inquiries in this branch of the investigation assigned to them, from a persuasion that the information elicited in reference to this subject will be regarded with more than ordinary interest by every one accustomed to measure, with a practised eye, the movement of public sentiment and feeling; and they have also been actuated in giving the foregoing exposition from a deep and pervading sense of the solemn responsibility under which they lie in having had committed to them a subject which, in their view, yields to no other of past or present time, in * 151 reference to * the varied, extensive, and all-absorbing interests involved in its decision. They regard the ultimate result of the proposed measure, as one which, if the measure be now adopted and carried forward by the Legislature of this Commonwealth, and if it be countenanced and carried into execution by the Executive of the United States, and eventually concurred in by the different powers who may be invited to cooperate to that end, will eventually confer on Massachusetts, on the United States, and on the age in which it is achieved, a renown whose duration will be coeval with the existence of our race. With this inadequate view of the subject, the Committee unanimously recommend the following resolutions, for the adoption of the Legislature.

Per order of the Committee.

STEPHEN FAIRBANKS, *Chairman.*

Commonwealth of Massachusetts.

In the year one thousand eight hundred and thirty-seven.

Resolves in relation to a Congress of Nations.

Resolved, That the resort to war, to settle questions of national profit or honor, is a practice derived from the barbarism of former ages, and inconsistent with the enlightened philanthropy of the present, still more adverse to the benign principles of Christianity, productive of extensive distractions, misery and corruptions, and usually inefficient for the purposes for which it is commenced, and hence it is incumbent on all civilized communities to devise measures for its suppression.

Resolved, That the institution of a Congress or Court of Nations appears to be, at present, the best practical method by which the disputes between nations can be adjusted, and the appeal to arms avoided.

Resolved, That it be recommended to the Executive of the United States, to open a negotiation with such other governments as, in its wisdom, it may deem proper, with a view to effect so important an arrangement.

Resolved, That His Excellency the Governor of this Commonwealth be requested to transmit a copy of this Report, and the accompanying Resolutions, to the President of the United States, and to the Executive of each of the States, to be communicated to the Legislatures of the several States, inviting their expression of sentiment and cooperation in favor of the end in view.

* 152   * In searching the records of the General Court of the State of Massachusetts, I find the following resolves, passed in 1838, of which I was ignorant before, and add them in this place.

Commonwealth of Massachusetts.

In the year of our Lord one thousand eight hundred and thirty-eight.

Resolves in relation to a Congress of Nations.

Resolved, That offensive war is incompatible with the true spirit of Christianity.

Resolved, That the great importance of the subject renders it the duty of all civilized communities to unite in the adoption of any practicable plan, calculated to effect so noble an object as the abolition of war, and the preservation of peace among the nations of the earth.

Resolved, That the institution of a Congress of Nations for the purpose of framing a code of international law, and establishing a high court of arbitration for the settlement of controversies between nations, is a scheme worthy of the careful attention and consideration of all enlightened governments.

Resolved, That His Excellency the Governor of this Commonwealth be requested to transmit a copy of these resolves, with the accompanying report, to the President of the United States, and to the Executive of each of the States, to be communicated to their respective Legislatures, inviting their cooperation in the proposed object.

House of Representatives, April 25, 1838.—Passed.

ROBERT C. WINTHROP, *Speaker.*

In Senate, April 25, 1838.—Passed.

MYRON LAWRENCE, *President.*

April 25, 1838.—Approved.

EDWARD EVERETT.

No. 7.

* 153 * *First Petition to Congress, presented by the New York Peace Society, the American Peace Society, the Vermont Peace Society, and many other individuals, the members of no peace society.*

To the Honorable, the Senate and House of Representatives of the United States of America, in Congress assembled on the first Monday in December, 1837.

The undersigned, members of the New York Peace Society, and other individuals friendly to the Peace cause, respectfully present the following Petition:

That your honorable body accede to the proposition of the Mexican Congress, as couched in the following terms, contained in a decree of that Congress dated May 20th, 1837, to wit:

"The government is hereby authorized to compromise the claims which the government of the United States has instituted, or may hereafter institute; and those in which they cannot agree may be submitted to the decision of a friendly power, the United States of America agreeing thereto."

Your petitioners feel, that it would greatly derogate from the high character hitherto sustained by this republic, to decline so honorable a proposal as that contained in the foregoing article; and, on the other hand, that it would redound to its highest honor, promptly and frankly to comply with it.

It is a universally admitted proposition, that a disinterested party is more likely to decide impartially in relation to a dispute, than the parties interested; and it is for this reason that men in their social capacity have consented to the establishment of judicial tribunals, to which to refer such of their individual disputes as they cannot satisfactorily adjust between themselves. For the same reason, in the opinion of your petitioners, ought international disputes of a similar kind to be referred to a disinterested party. And they are the more encouraged to hope, that this petition will be favorably received by your honorable body, from the consideration of the fact, that the principle of arbitration has been adopted by the government of the United States in several instances already, whereby the soundness of that principle has been clearly recognized, and its compatibility with the honor, dignity, and rights of the nation virtually admitted.

   Your petitioners take this opportunity to pray your honorable body to
* 154 adopt the principle of reference to a third party of such international * disputes as cannot be amicably adjusted by the parties themselves, as an *invariable* rule of action, instead of an *occasional* one. They can see no possible reason why it should not be the rule at all times, as well as on particular occasions. There is *no time* that a party to a dispute is not less likely to decide impartially in relation to its merits, than a disinterested party would be; and, consequently, there is *always* the same reason why parties, whether individual or international, should refer to arbitration such disputes as they are unable to adjust amicably between themselves.

Your petitioners would further pray your honorable body, in pursuance of this principle, to send forth a proposal to the various governments of the world, to unite with your honorable body in the establishment of a great international board of arbitration, or a Congress of Nations, to which to refer international disputes; and, also, for the purpose of digesting and preparing a regular code of international law, obligatory on such nations as may afterwards adopt it.

If the principle of arbitration is to become the order of the day, then there can be no question as to the best mode; and if there is to be a law of nations at all, it is equally clear with regard to the propriety of its being embodied in a regular code. No government, engrossed with its own affairs, can devote the time requisite to the thorough examination of the various international disputes; and hence the necessity for the appointment of a board of arbitrators for the purpose, who would be able to devote to the business their undivided attention. And besides this, a board of arbitrators, composed of delegates from various nations, would, by containing within itself a counterpoise of interests, be more likely to give an impartial decision, than would any single government. With regard to the formation of a code of international law, all the reasons that can be assigned for the *enactment* of law in general, are equally applicable to the enactment of an international code. The principles of law need to be settled and defined. For want of this, in the case of the law of nations, many wars have occurred. And who so suitable to prepare an international code of law, as an international tribunal of the kind contemplated? Assuredly, it is not competent for *one nation* to decide what shall be the law for *all the nations of the world,* in their intercourse with one another. Nothing short of *an international tribunal* is, in the opinion of your petitioners, competent to the preparation of an *international code of law*—and competent to the explication and application of that law, after its enactment, in cases of *international dispute*. And yet, your petitioners do not propose a measure which would be any infringement, even the least, on the
* 155 independence and sovereignty of nations. As they have * already hinted, they propose only, that this law shall be obligatory on those nations that may adopt it, after its enactment by the tribunal.

Nor do your petitioners propose, that that tribunal be clothed with power *to enforce* its decisions, but that it rely for its efficiency solely on the impartiality and correctness of those decisions, and the honor and justice of the parties concerned. And when your petitioners consider the tenacity with which nations adhere to the point of honor, and that they never embark in war without a plausible excuse, they are forced to the conclusion, that *a righteous* decision of an international dispute, emanating from an authorized, international tribunal, in accordance with an international code of law, accompanied by the reasons for that decision, and appealing solely to national honor and justice, could not fail to meet with a favorable reception by the parties. To suppose otherwise, would be to suppose, that those vast portions of mankind denominated nations, that stand so much on their dignity and honor, have less pretension to those noble qualities, than have two common citizens who refer a dispute to arbitrators in the ordinary concerns of private life, and who would consider themselves eternally disgraced, were they to disregard a fair decision. Indeed, to suppose that nations would not heed a decision of the kind, would be an impeachment of their high character, and an insult to their fair fame.

But your petitioners do not stake their cause on the *certainty* of the efficiency of the plan proposed. They would say, that if there is even a *tendency* in the scheme to prevent such an evil as war, nations ought to adopt it. Nay, they will go further, and say, that if there is a remote probability of its preventing *a single* war; yea, if it is not demonstrable that it will have no tendency to prevent war; nations ought to *make trial* of it, to say the least. The nation refusing to participate in such an attempt at the pacification of the world, would manifest no desire to avoid war, and could no longer denominate it its last resort. On the other hand, should the trial of the scheme be made, and even prove abortive, nations will not have labored in vain: they will thereby have manifested some disposition to avoid war, and could then with some appearance of truth denominate it their last resort—which otherwise they could not do.

Your petitioners feel desirous, that this country should not only combine with others in promoting the great and glorious scheme under consideration, but that she should lead the way, by sending forth the GREAT PROPOSAL for a Congress of Nations, to the various nations of the earth. They would fain see their own country stand forth in advance of all others in this great, this glorious, this

heaven-born enterprise, presenting to the admiring view of the whole uni-
* 156   verse a * spectacle of moral grandeur and sublimity unequalled in the

career of nations, and entitled to imperishable renown. Fain would they see the names of their rulers inscribed on the same page of immortality with those of a Numa Pompilius, an Antoninus Pius, a Leopold of Lorraine, a Walpole, a Fleury, a Maximilian II, a Rudolph II, a Ferdinand VI, a Robert I, and a William Penn, and not on that page of infamy crimsoned with human blood.

Your petitioners would be among the last, to base their cause on any ground but that of its own intrinsic merits. Nevertheless, it is always gratifying to the friends of a good cause, to know that it has the countenance and support of the wise and the good.

[Here follow extracts from the first and second report of the Legislature of Massachusetts, which it is unnecessary to repeat.]

Your Petitioners also find the sage Franklin holding language like the following: "We daily make great improvements in *natural*, there is one I wish to see in *moral*, philosophy;—the discovery of a plan that would induce and oblige nations to settle their disputes, without first cutting one another's throats. When will human nature be sufficiently improved to see the advantage of this?" "Wonderful," says the illustrious Jefferson, "has been the progress of human improvement in other respects. Let us hope, then, that the law of nature, which makes virtuous conduct produce benefit, and vice loss, to the agent, in the long run; which has sanctioned the common principle that honesty is the best policy, will in time influence the proceedings of nations as well as individuals; that we shall at length be sensible, that war is an instrument entirely inefficient toward redressing wrong; that it multiplies, instead of indemnifying losses. These truths are *palpable*, and *must*, in the progress of time, have their influence on the minds and conduct of nations."

But your petitioners forbear from further quotation. Enough has been produced to show, that were the rulers of the world such men as our Franklins and Jeffersons, this project would not want supporters. And could those venerable, patriot sages revisit the earth, and once more take their seats in the American Congress, we doubt not that they would be among the foremost to rise up in your midst, and advocate the adoption of the measure recommended in this petition. May we not hope, that your honorable body will, by the adoption of a similar course, prove yourselves in this respect a Congress of Franklins and Jeffersons—a Congress of sages and philanthropists—a Congress acting for the highest interests, not of a single nation at a particular period, but of the whole human family henceforth to the end of time?

*157 That the custom of war has hitherto prevailed, is no reason for its * longer continuance. We of the present generation claim to live in an age of superior light, in which customs are brought to the test of reason. This touchstone needs but to be applied to the custom of war, to procure at once its abolition. It is a custom altogether unsuited to the high state of civilization of the present period. Time it is, that some general movement were made among the nations, to bring it to a termination. Suffice it to have outlived customs far less barbarous, which have disappeared before the bright beams of civilization, like the mists of morning before the ascending sun. Too long has this hydra been permitted to rear his horrid crests amid scenes of civilization and refinement. Too long have the nations of Christendom, professing to be governed by a peaceful religion, been subjected by their warlike policy to the taunts of the Jew, the scorn of the Mussulman, and the reproach of the heathen. The rulers of Christendom owe it to themselves, they owe it to the religion they profess, they owe it to the human race, to change at once and for ever their international policy, by the adoption of a pacific mode of adjusting international disputes. Nor can they, with all the light that is blazing on them, any longer forbear to adopt such a measure, without incurring the most awful guilt. War that is not indeed the last resort, is wholesale murder; and until every probable expedient has been resorted to, to prevent it, it is not the last resort. Your petitioners, therefore, feel, that unless the governments of the world, and especially of Christendom, will make a sincere trial of the principle of arbitration for the adjustment of their disputes, and thereby bring its efficiency to the full test, they cannot embark in war without guilt of the most fearful magnitude, and the deepest die—THE GUILT OF THE BLOOD OF NATIONS! And they further feel, that it would not only be an immortal honor to the government that might move first in this great undertaking, by making a proposition of the kind to others, but that no government is justifiable in waiting for another to make the first movement. And, finally, they feel that the government of this country, above all others, is under obligation to be the foremost in this instance. Our institutions, our policy, the genius of our country, our high pretensions to superiority in all that is great and ennobling, demand it at our hands. And your petitioners do most fervently hope, that your honorable body will not turn a deaf ear to the call, but that, by your timely and favorable action in the case, you will prove to the world that all these claims to transcendent excellence are not in vain.

No. 8.

* 158   *Report on the foregoing Petition.*

Mr. LEGARE, from the Committee on Foreign Affairs, made the following REPORT:

The Committee on Foreign Affairs, to whom was referred the memorial of the New York Peace Society, and other individuals friendly to the peace cause, report as follows:

The prayer of the memoralists is twofold. They desire, in the first place, that our differences with Mexico should be referred to the arbitration of a third power. The House is already informed that, to this extent, their petition has been answered and fulfilled by the Executive—our claims upon that government having, at the instance of the latter, been submitted to an umpire of its own choosing. So far, therefore, as the object of the memorialists was to bring about this practical result in a public interest of great importance and pressing exigency, it has been accomplished, no doubt, to their entire satisfaction.

But they do not stop here. They proceed to recommend to Congress that it "adopt the principle of reference to a third power of such international disputes as cannot be amicably adjusted by the parties themselves, as an invariable rule of action, instead of an occasional one." And they further pray that, " in pursuance of this principle, a proposal be sent forth by this government to those of other nations, that they would unite with it in the establishment of a great international *board of arbitration,* or a *Congress of Nations,* to which to refer international disputes, and also for the purpose of digesting and preparing *a regular code of international law,* obligatory on such nations as may afterwards adopt it." They think that this board of arbitrators should be composed of delegates from various nations, and that to this board should be confided the forming a code of international law.

It is proper to observe, however, that they do not propose this code "shall be binding upon any nations which may not willingly adopt it, after its enactment by the tribunal;" nor do they propose that that tribunal be clothed with power to *enforce* its decisions; but that it shall rely for its efficiency solely on the impartiality and correctness of those decisions, and the honor and justice of the parties concerned.

The petitioners conclude, by expressing a desire that this country should not only combine with others in what they characterize as "the great and * 159 glorious scheme under consideration," but that they "should * lead the way, by sending forth the proposal for a Congress of Nations" to the various governments of the civilized world.

The Committee have been earnestly pressed to take this latter prayer of the petitioners into consideration, and to make a direct, full, and solemn report, both upon its principles and its practicability. It is in compliance with a desire thus entertained in many respectable quarters, that they have the honor of submitting to the House the following reflections:

The Committee need scarcely say that they fully appreciate and sympathize with the philanthropic feelings and purposes expressed in the memorial. They agree that the union of all nations, in a state of peace, under the restraints and the protection of law, is the ideal perfection of civil society. Not, however, that they would be understood as affirming that war has always, in the history of mankind, been an unmixed or uncompensated evil. They do not think so. To say nothing of the heroic virtues which are formed under its stern discipline, and exercised by its trials and perils, war has, in fact, been often, both in ancient and in modern times, a mighty and even a necessary instrument of civilization. It is sufficient, in this connection, barely to mention the names of Alexander and Charlemagne. But the Committee also think that those times are gone by. Far other agents of amelioration and progress are at work now— agents infinitely more powerful in their quiet and silent, but incessant operation, and whose efficacy would be greatly impaired by war, did they not tend, more than any thing else, to supersede and put an end to it. The age is reproached with being a mechanical and ignoble one—with its sordid love of gain, its plodding devotion to business, and its preference of physical comforts and personal accommodation, to objects that elevate the imagination and refine the taste in art and literature. This reproach is, no doubt, to a certain degree, well founded; but we must not forget that we do not forego (as far as we do) the advantages referred to, without a real, and, in the eye of sober reason, an abundantly adequate compensation. It is true that the most peculiar characteristic of the civilization of these times is a demand, becoming universal among all classes of society, for the various physical comforts, of which commerce is the inexhaustible source. But it is this very peculiarity that opens an entirely new prospect to the human race, and makes the present moment an epoch in its history. This commercial or economical civilization, if we may call it so, is reconstructing society

on the broadest and most solid basis. It is essentially democratic in its character and tendencies. It pursues steadily, and achieves, with more and
* 160 more success every day, the greatest good of the greatest * number. It
is every where increasing population, and adding immensely to the fund
that employs and rewards labor. In spite of many disturbing causes, which will
disappear in the progress of things, it is elevating the poor in the social scale,
providing for them better food, raiment and lodging, as well as means of a suitable
moral and intellectual education. It is bringing the most distant families of
mankind, as it were, into contact with one another, and effacing all the sharp and
salient peculiarities of national character that now estrange them from each
other. It is revealing the great cardinal truth of free trade—so pregnant with
moral as well as political results—that " self-love and social are the same; "
that every country is interested in the prosperity of every other; that production
can never be excessive, because, where exchanges are untrammeled, it produces
its own consumption; that nothing, in short, can be more shallow in science, as
well as sordid and narrow in spirit, than a restrictive policy founded upon the
idea that a nation can only enrich itself at the expense of its neighbors, or
has any thing to gain, in the long run, from their losses. When we reflect that,
during the whole of the last century, and for a considerable period before, the
far greater part of the blood and treasure so prodigally lavished in almost
incessant war, was a sacrifice, directly or indirectly, to fallacious views of commercial monopoly and colonial dominion considered as instrumental to that
monopoly, we shall fully appreciate the importance of this simple truth, once
become, as it will infallibly become, a settled maxim of national policy. With
notions of economy and personal comfort, such as are made the reproach of the
times, mankind are not likely much longer to acquiesce in the wanton and prof-
ligate waste of their resources, of the means of so much private and public
prosperity, in contests which—to say nothing of the unspeakable evils that
accompany them—cannot possibly result in any adequate advantage to either
party. Their reluctance to take up arms will be increased by a regard not only
to their own interest directly, but to that of their adversaries, which is in
effect the same thing; to make war upon their customers in trade, will be felt
to be a mischievous and suicidal insanity. This motive is, perhaps, not a
romantic one; but it is not the less powerful for addressing itself less to
sentiment and the imagination than to the habitual selfishness of human nature.
It is thus that physical causes are producing moral effects of the greatest importance, and that political economy becomes the most effective auxiliary of
Christianity. We already see, in a manner not to be mistaken, the influence of
such ideas in the contemporary history of Europe, although they are just
beginning to take hold of the public mind, and there are so many obstacles
* 161 to their progress in the actual * state of things there. It is scarcely possible to imagine a greater revolution of opinion, in the same time, than has
occurred since the peace of 1815. A single generation is not yet passed away
since the downfall of Napoleon, and his military despotism begins already to
strike the minds of men as a barbarous anomaly in such an age. Since the last

French revolution, causes of controversy, without number, sufficient to have produced desolating wars at any previous epoch, have arisen and passed away without occasioning one, except the disputed succession in Spain—an exception that proves the rule. Much is due, no doubt, to the personal character and enlightened views of those whose position enabled them to control that great event; but, let it be remembered that that character and those views were themselves the work of the age which they reflect so faithfully.

The Committee will add, that there is another point in which every thing that tends to preserve the peace of nations will, ere-long, come to be universally regarded as peculiarly interesting to mankind: they allude to its effect in promoting the great cause of limited or constitutional government. War has ever been the most fruitful source of arbitrary power. They are, indeed, to a certain extent, inseparable. A military is, necessarily, in spirit and effect, a despotic, and must generally be a monarchical organization. Not only so, but the evil tends to propagate and to perpetuate itself. One great power arming for conquest compels all neighboring powers to arm for defence; and it is not a vain or fanciful saying, that laws are silent amidst the din of arms. The instinct of self-preservation is at least as strong in nations as in individuals. They ever have been, and ever will be, ready to sacrifice, without scruple, their dearest rights and liberties in order to maintain their national independence. The yoke of the foreigner is so galling and degrading, that there is no other which mankind are not willing to bear in order to avoid it. "The salvation of the people,"—*salus populi,*— at whatever cost or risk, must and will be the supreme law, under every form of government. The dictators of republican Rome, the terrible despotism of the executive committees of the French Convention, are only instances of a universal law of society and of human nature under such circumstances. Hence the impossibility, for the present at least, of maintaining such institutions as ours on the continent of Europe.

Mirabeau embodied the whole philosophy of the subject in his well-known apothegm, that France was "geographically monarchical." The federal relations of Europe (for Europe *is*, in fact, a confederacy) admit, in *strict theory*, of no
          arbiter but the sword; and the independence of most of the powers has
* 162   been preserved—as far as it has been pre-*served at all—at the cost of
          popular liberty. That happy compromise by which the wisdom of our
fathers—availing itself, it is true, of such circumstances as have never occurred elsewhere—has reconciled, on this continent, the sovereignty of the States with the rights of individuals, under a peaceful, judicial administration of the law, is still, and is likely long to continue, a *desideratum* there. But the spirit of the age is gradually becoming more favorable to such institutions, just in proportion as it is becoming less disposed to war. Peace is the hope of liberty—peace, consecrated as the standing, fundamental policy of the world. Such a state of opinion, or such a condition of things as will dispense with large armies and military discipline, with a power, in effect dictatorial, in the executive department of governments, and with the ambition, the glory, and the fatal popularity and influence of successful generals; such a perpetual and perfect intercourse, commercial

and otherwise, among men as will mitigate extremely, if not extinguish, all mutual jealousy and hostility between nations destined, under the blessed influences of Christian civilization, to form but one great family, and will thus deprive politicians of the occasion of turning the wildest frenzy and worst calamities of mankind into a means of sanctifying the abuses of government—will inevitably lead, in this age, to the general establishment of representative institutions. All the tendencies of commerce and industry are to social equality; peace will add to that equality rational liberty under a government of laws; and both will tend to perpetuate, by a natural reaction, the causes that produced them.

Concurring thus fully in the benevolent objects of the memorialists, and believing that there is a visible tendency in the spirit and institutions of the age towards the practical accomplishment of it at some future period, the Committee regret to have to say that they have not the same confidence in the *means* recommended in the petition. They are of opinion that reforms so fundamental, can only be brought about by the gradual progress of civilization, and in consequence of a real change in the condition of society. They must follow events, and conform to them; they cannot, by any contrivance of man, be made to precede and control them. All attempts, in such matters, except by bloody revolutions or conquests, to anticipate the natural course of things, are entirely unavailing.

The scheme of the memorialists is, as we have seen, to refer all international disputes to a Congress of deputies, and to authorize that Congress to digest a code of public law that shall be binding only on such powers as should voluntarily adopt it.

The first objection to this plan lies upon the surface, and is entirely * 163 * fatal. The unanimous consent of nations, in the actual state of the world, to such a proposal, is—as any one will be convinced who reflects a moment upon their political relations, or will but cast his eye over a map of Europe—entirely out of the question; and the refusal of a single great power to acquiesce in it, would alone render it abortive. This is not matter of speculation; it is what has actually occurred in one of the most important departments of international law. The House is aware that Great Britain maintains doctrines in reference to the maritime rights of belligerents, which were formally disavowed and denounced, during the war of our Revolution, by almost all the leading powers of Europe, banded together to resist the enforcement of them in practice. On some of the points involved in the declarations of the Armed Neutrality, our own prize courts have followed, perhaps too implicitly, those of England; but on others—for example, the rule, as it is called, of '56—they have adhered to the law, as explained by that famous league. And yet, against the concurring opinions of all the rest of the civilized world, and in spite of the bloody wars to which the exercise of her pretended rights has led, and may yet lead, Great Britain maintains her principles, irreconcilable as they are with the practice of nations in analogous cases on land, and indeed with all modern ideas of civilized warfare; and even interposes her overruling influence to prevent any of the minor states of Europe from adopting, for their own convenience, provisions inconsistent with those principles, in treaties professedly confined to the parties making them.

What declaration of a Congress, constituted as the one in question would be, can be expected to have, by the mere weight of its authority, more effect on the opinions and the conduct of mankind, than that of such a formidable coalition as the Armed Neutrality?

Had England not engrossed the empire of the seas for about a century past, it is scarcely possible to doubt but that the law of maritime captures would have been made to correspond more strictly with the analogies of war on land, and private property been held as sacred in the one case as in the other. It is worthy of notice, that at the Congress of Utrecht, before her ascendant was established, that power was an advocate of the rights of neutrals. She is now their worst enemy; and her resistance presents an obstacle, for the present at least, quite insuperable to any reform in this particular; just as the refusal of either France, or Austria, or Russia, &c., would be fatal to the project of the memorialists. Such is the preponderance of these powers in the balance of Europe, so peculiar and so various their interests, so many changes will be necessary in most of them to bring their institutions into harmony with the leveling * 164 spirit of the age, and so to make it all * safe for them to submit to any arbiter but force, that it were chimerical to expect their cooperation in any plan to dispense with it altogether. When Henry IV conceived *his* project of perpetual peace, he did not look for the countenance or consent of the then predominant house of Austria. On the contrary, his first object was to overcome the resistance which he expected from that quarter. His grand scheme of pacification was founded on as vast a one of preparatory war and revolution. That house was to be reduced; its power broken; its territory partitioned. This was evidently an indispensable prerequisite, and his was too practical a mind not to perceive it. The Committee will add here, what will be found to illustrate another proposition advanced in this report, that his project assumed a still more important alteration in the interests and relations of mankind. It constituted Europe on an entirely new basis. He would have built up a balance of power on something like an equality of territory. He would have dealt with that continent as an ancient lawgiver—a Moses or Lycurgus—would have dealt with the soil of a particular country, distributing it on agrarian principles, in order that his new constitution of society should have something solid to rest upon in the nature of things. In this respect, too, as the Committee will presently endeavor to show, he evinced a practical wisdom far above such a dream as that of a revolution in the whole conduct of nations, to be effected by a mere declaration of abstract principles on paper or parchment.

And this leads to the second objection, which is, that even if the consent of all the great powers—supposing their present relations toward one another to remain precisely as they are—could be obtained to such an experiment, there seems to your Committee to be no reason for anticipating any good result from either of the expedients recommended by the memorialists.

First: with regard to a code of international law. Nothing, in the opinion of your Committee, is more fallacious than the idea that mere positive legislation, when not preceded or accompanied by conquest or revolution, has ever had a very important agency in human affairs. This proposition, they are aware, may seem paradoxical at a period when so much is said about written codes and constitutions; but it is fully established by experience, even were it not, as it is, sufficiently clear *a priori*. The most renowned systems of legislation have been the slow work of time, modified in some degree, and improved by an enlightened, experimental wisdom, taking advantage of circumstances, rather than aspiring to control them. Even when reduced to the form of codes, they have done little more, when they have done any good at all, than record with precision, * 165 and clothe in solemn form, the opinions, * usages and manners of a people, with such limited modifications of them as have been just alluded to. The Committee will not trouble the House with the elaborate development to which the importance of this great and fundamental truth would, on a proper occasion, so fully entitle it; nor by citing examples which it would be easy to multiply, to confirm and illustrate it. But there is one of these, too often mentioned to be overlooked, too striking to be slighted, and yet in general so little understood as to require a statement of the precise truth in regard to it: they mean the Justinian collection, which is habitually cited as an instance of written law, properly so called, that is, of law arbitrarily prescribed by the supreme power in the state; yet every civilian knows that the great bulk and body of the *corpus juris civilis* is strictly *common law*, the law, namely, of opinion, of interpretation, and of practice. The Pandects are, from beginning to end, nothing but a repository of the wisdom of the great jurisconsults of a better age, delivered to the public in the shape of treatises, institutes and maxims, or in that of consultations or opinions solving questions of practical jurisprudence.

But if this be true even of the law of property and contract (*meum* and *tuum*), it is obviously still more applicable to public law in both its great branches, the constitutional and the international, but especially the latter. As to constitutions, the experience of the last half century supersedes the necessity of saying a word about their total inefficacy where a people is not ripe for them; or, in other words, where they are arbitrarily made for a people. Such an instrument is a mere deception, not worth the parchment on which it is engrossed. None but the most visionary minds can now have any faith in the mysteries, once held in such reverence, of written forms. Our own government has been absurdly cited as an example of the kind. It is, as the House is aware, a remarkable instance of the very reverse. Its two prominent characteristics, its two vital principles as a federal republic—the popular representation in one branch of the legislature, the equality of voices in the other—are founded on *facts*, of which the existence is quite independent of all constitutions, and which may be considered as primordial in this country. The States were as free, even as republican before the Revolution, as they are now; they were at the same time, independent communities, connected, indeed, by many ties, but especially by geographical position and by their common relation to the mother country, but still distinct and independent of each other. It might have been predicted with confidence, that no government could be formed which should not * 166 reconcile, as far as possible, both these * facts. Washington, for example, as is very apparent from his correspondence, as well as from his conduct, had, with that sound good sense and large, comprehensive and practical wisdom so characteristic of him, a clear perception of this truth. The form of the Legislative Assembly, composed of two Houses, was the established one of the country— a part of its common law and hereditary liberties, and those of the whole English race: but *how* were those Houses to be constituted? Here was a new question, and the only new question; and yet the solution of it, in the very manner in which it was solved, was inevitable. No one can imagine, that on any merely theoretical principles the State of Virginia could have been brought then, or the State of New York could be brought now, for the first time, to consent that her immense numerical superiority should be neutralized in the equal vote of the Senate. So far, however, from being the strange anomaly which a foreigner might imagine it, it is the most natural thing in the world; so far from being an arbitrary institution it is, so to express it, a corollary flowing out of our whole history; instead of being the creature of the constitution, it was its necessary, indispensable condition. Nor is it merely because it is recognized in that constitution, and clothed by it with a peculiar sanctity, that it maintains its place there; it rests on more solid ground—on public opinion. The spirit which produced it is still in all its pristine vigor; the fact, of which it was the expression, still exists; the States, one and all of them, have a deep interest in maintaining their independence as States, and would unite in resisting a change which would arm the strong against the weak, to the common ruin. The Senate is thus fully a counterpoise to the other House; because, like that House, it is the sign of a living power—the representative of an actual interest; because, like it, it is founded upon a state of opinion, and of things which cannot be changed without war—to maintain which, men would be willing to lay down their lives, and to sacrifice even the government itself. It is this that gives to the Senate of the United States more weight and efficiency than belong to any similar body, any House of Lords, or Chamber of Peers, in the world. But this unquestionable truth at the same time sufficiently evinces, that, of all chimeras, it is the wildest to expect to see similar institutions established, to any practical good purpose, in countries where there are *no facts* that answer to them.

But if codes or municipal and constitutional law, to be effective must mainly form themselves in the silent progress of events, we find in international law a body of jurisprudence which is, and of necessity must be, exclusively the growth of opinion. There is here no legislative power, no common arbiter, * 167 nothing but an occasional convention or * established usage, to give sanction to its precepts. And yet whoever, fresh from the history of mankind in more remote ages, shall open the great work of Grotius, will be struck with the immense progress of society, revealed in every page of it. This justly celebrated, and still, in its kind, unrivaled collection of the maxims of international justice, standing on the very threshold of what is properly called modern history, ought to be considered, perhaps, as the grandest monument which human hands have yet erected to the influence of Christianity. Before the 16th century, the conventional law of nations hardly deserves notice; treaties are but few and meagre: but Europe was a family of nations bound together in the unity of a common faith, and the law of enlightened reason and of good-will among men, proclaimed from the pulpit and at the altar, established itself, gradually and by tacit consent, in the practice of mankind. It is thus that most of the usages which give such a hideous and barbarous aspect to war, even in the most civilized periods of antiquity, have been effaced. Certainly, some additional reforms might be made in international law, as, for example, in the matter of maritime captures, to which allusion has already been had. These reforms, to the honor of our country be it said, have been incessantly aimed at and perseveringly pursued, in her negotiations, from the very first into which she entered as an independent nation, down to the present time. Your Committee trust that no administration will ever lose sight of them; they are confident of ultimate success; they have unlimited faith in the truth, justice, and wisdom of the maxims involved in these reforms; but it is only from the gradual progress of social improvement that such a consummation is to be hoped for. It is not a code or collection of these maxims that is wanted: it is the power to enforce or the spirit to practise them which no code can give.

With regard to the proposed international board of arbitration, the objections of the Committee are still stronger. A code digested and promulged as the memorialists desire, would do no good, but it could scarcely do any harm. Not so with a tribunal of any sort. The probability, to be sure, is, that the decrees of such a one as is here contemplated would be merely nugatory; but, if it had any influence at all, it might, in the actual relations of the great powers, easily be perverted to the worst ends. It might be made especially to impede the progress of the very improvements it would have been instituted to promote, and, instead of disarming the mighty, become in their hands an engine of usurpation and tyranny. He is but superficially versed in the history of nations who does not know that some of the greatest revolutions in society have been brought about through the instrumentality of judicial tribunals. The Committee * 168 will cite but one example: they refer to * the gradual subversion of the feudal confederacy of France, by the crown exercising, as it did, a paramount influence over a nominal court of peers. The authority of law, once established and acknowledged among men, is second only to that of religion. Judges do much more than pronounce and enforce judgment in particular cases; they shape the opinions of mankind in analogous ones; and those opinions, as we have seen, are the basis of all government and legislation.

It will immediately occur to the House, that the only republic in the world should be very careful not to commit its destinies, in any serious degree, to institutions which might and would be controlled by influences hostile to its principles; and, the more especially, as the natural tendency of things is more favorable to those principles than any *policy* shaped or controlled by the existing governments of Europe can possibly be expected to prove. In the nature of things, every organ, however constituted, of such governments, must speak the language of what is called "resistance" to the spirit of the age; and if any thing could enable them to resist that spirit, it would be a permanent Congress of Laybach or Verona, laying down the law of war and peace for all nations. This was, indeed, the very scheme of the Holy Alliance, to which this country was formally invited to accede.

The example of the Amphictyonic Council of Greece, which has been cited with confidence by the petitioners, is, in the opinion of the Committee, as unfavorable to their purpose as any that could be selected from the records of the past. Without going into a critical examination of its history, for which this is not a suitable occasion, it is sufficient to refer to indisputable general results, to what every one who will cast his eye, however carelessly, over the annals of those commonwealths, will at once perceive—that it had no effect whatever in healing their fatal dissensions; that so long as there was any thing like a balance of power among the principal states, they continued to make war upon each other, without the least regard to the imaginary jurisdiction of that assembly; that, although by its constitution the twelve peoples composing it had each an equal voice in it, whatever might be their inequality of weight and importance, yet its decisions were continually and openly swayed by the influence of the power or powers in the ascendant for the time being; and finally, that it was by availing himself of his absolute control over it, and by taking advantage of a favorable juncture in affairs brought about by its policy, that Philip of Macedon found a plausible pretext, and a show of legitimate authority, to sanctify the machinations which he had been long contriving, and the war which he ultimately waged with success against the liberties of Greece.

* 169   * Every other mere confederation, both in ancient and modern times, except under circumstances so peculiar as to make them unfit to be considered as precedents, has been attended with the same results. Either the leading members of them, at the head of standing, systematic parties, have been at perpetual war with each other, or the overruling ascendant of some one of them has enabled it to invade the rights of all the rest, in every form of violence and artifice. The late German empire, for example, affords us instances of both these tendencies. Some of the longest and most desolating wars that have scourged Europe have grown out of the conflicting interests of the members of that league of peace, and had for their avowed object the adjustment of those interests according to the true theory of its public law. This was as much the case after as before the treaty of Westphalia, although one capital object of that memorable negotiation was to reform the constitution or the administration of the Imperial Chamber and the Aulic Council—in which jurisdiction in federal and feudal causes had been vested, without any effect, however, in deciding them to the satisfaction of the weaker party. Neither ought it to be forgotten, that by that treaty a majority of suffrages in the diet was no longer to give the law in any matters that related to religion, or in which the two great parties, as such, should vote differently, or, in general, in any case wherein all the states could not be considered as forming a single consolidated nation. In all such cases, the questions submitted to them were to be treated as those arising between foreign nations, and to be arranged by compromise, with no appeal but to the sword. So difficult is it to accomplish what the memorialists propose,—

the peaceful decision of controversies between states whose interests are materially different,—that even where tribunals have been instituted for that purpose, the abuses to which they have been made to lend their authority have seldom failed, in the end, to aggravate and multiply the very evils they were intended to prevent. Experience shows, that of all wars, the most obstinate and terrible are those which grow out of such abuses. They partake of the nature of revolution and civil war; the color of authority on the one side, the sense of injustice on the other, inflame the usual bitterness of hostility; and battles are more sanguinary, and victory less merciful, where the contest is waged by parties standing towards each other in the supposed relation of rebel and tyrant. Such institutions, therefore, unless where the circumstances of a country are very peculiar, have inevitably one of two effects: they either strengthen the hands of the oppressor, or they lead to dreadful and * 170 desolating wars to overthrow him; sometimes, as in * the case of the Germanic empire, and the house of Austria in the seventeenth century, to both.

Upon the whole, your Committee are of opinion that time is the best reformer in such things, and that any attempt to anticipate the natural progress of events, by institutions arbitrarily adopted, would either be vain, or something worse than vain. They have endeavored to show that the cause of peace is visibly gaining ground; that mankind are already become, and will daily become more and more indisposed to sacrifice their comforts and their business to the ambition of governments; nay, that governments themselves, partaking of the spirit of the times, or dreading its effects, avoid, as much as possible, those ruinous contests by which nations are rendered discontented, and rulers more dependent on them, just when suffering and poverty most dispose them to revolt. Instead of Congresses to put an end to war, generally on the foot of the *statu quo ante bellum*, there are Congresses to prevent a rupture, and piles of protocols attest that power, as was said of the Spartans after a memorable defeat, has lost much of its insolent and peremptory brevity of speech. The truth is, that every war hereafter will, by the social disorders that are likely to accompany or to follow such an event, throw additional obstacles in the way of future ones. The sword will thus prove the surest guaranty of peace.

Your Committee, therefore, do not think the establishment of a permanent international tribunal, under the present circumstances of the world, at all desirable; but they heartily concur with the memorialists in recommending a reference to a third power of all such controversies as can safely be confided to any tribunal unknown to the constitution of our own country. Such a practice will be followed by other powers, already inclined, as we have seen, to avoid war, and will soon grow up into the customary law of civilized nations. They conclude, therefore, by recommending to the memorialists to persevere in exerting whatever influence they may possess over public opinion, to dispose it habitually to the accommodation of national differences without bloodshed; and to the House, the adoption of the following resolution:

Resolved, That the Committee be discharged from the further consideration of the subject referred to them.

No. 9.

*171   *Second Petition of the American Peace Society to Congress.

To the Honorable Senate and House of Representatives of the United States of America, in Congress assembled:

The undersigned, President and Executive Committee of the American Peace Society, by the authority and in behalf of that Society, present the following memorial and petition:

Believing that the custom of war between Christian nations is barbarous and unnecessary, and, to quote the language of the illustrious Jefferson, " that war is an instrument entirely inefficient toward redressing wrong, and that it multiplies instead of indemnifying losses; " and being fully assured, that the time has at length come, when a more cheap, humane, equitable and Christian method of settling international contests may be obtained, we petition your honorable bodies to take such means as may appear to your wisdom best adapted to this desirable end.

The plan which your petitioners would venture to suggest, as best adapted to bring about so desirable a consummation, is simple and easy to be accomplished. It consists of two distinct parts, either of which may be accomplished without the other; but their practicability and utility would be promoted by the union of both.

1. A Congress of Ambassadors representing such of the governments of Christendom as shall unite in the measure, for the purpose of digesting a code of international law, to be adopted by the universal consent of the Congress, voting by nations, and binding only on the governments that shall freely adopt it. When this work is carried as far as the circumstances of the times will permit, the Congress may be dissolved, or adjourned *sine die*, to be reassembled when circumstances favorable to a further amelioration of the condition of man may be developed.

2. An international tribunal, consisting of eminent civilians, appointed by the government of each of the concurring powers, to hold their offices during good behaviour, who shall judge all cases brought before them by the mutual consent of any two or more nations, to hold their sessions in any of the countries of the high contracting parties, except in the territory of either of the parties appealing to them for judgment, who shall base their decisions on the abovementioned code of laws, so far as it is settled, and when that fails, on the prin-
*172 ciples of *equity; such judgments to be enforced only by the power of public opinion, and such other peaceful means as the nations shall adopt by their ambassadors in Congress assembled.

Your petitioners are aware, that the progress of such a Congress would be slow, but the results would be the more permanent and valuable. It would begin by adopting those principles which are almost self-evident, and would advance to those which are more doubtful and complicated. Experience has shown on moral subjects, no less than in the exact sciences, that when first principles have been firmly established, the most complicated propositions may be demonstrated, and also when people once heartily begin to promote a good work, that a spirit of mutual concession is generated, which will make crooked things straight, remove mountains of difficulty, and fill up intervening valleys;— which truth our own country, both under the old confederation and the new constitution, has abundantly exemplified.

It is not long since the world was ruled altogether by the sword, but now, " opinion is the queen of the world," * and begins to extend her legitimate sway over the nations of the earth. Her power will increase as civilization extends, and the march of civilization is commensurate with the duration of peace and the extent of peace principles. It is the gospel of peace which will " rebuke strong nations afar off," and compel them by the power of public opinion to " beat their swords into ploughshares, and their spears into pruning-hooks." †

We live in an age when the bare attempt to do that which ought to be done, insures success. The speed, with which great enterprises are carried to their successful consummation, is no more to be measured by the creeping pace of public opinion in by-gone ages, than the velocity of a railroad car is to be judged by the slow movements of the cumbersome wains of antiquity.

If ancient attempts to preserve peace by an international tribunal, were only partially successful, that ought not to discourage us from making similar attempts on a larger scale, and in a more mature state of society, any more than the entire failure, or only partial success, of former attempts at a steam-boat, ought to have discouraged Fulton. The partial success of the Old Confederation, formed for the government of the Union in 1775, in a time of war, excitement, and inexperience in the art of self-government, did not discourage the framers of the New Constitution in 1787; but it must be confessed, that the Old Con- * 173 federation was the parent of the New Constitution, and had not * *that* existed, *this* could never have been born. The framers of the New Constitution profited by the errors of their predecessors, and produced an institution which has astonished and delighted the world. All improvement is, in its very nature, progressive. Let the present generation form a confederation of Christian nations for desirable purposes,—the next generation will produce a constitution which, while it will leave every nation perfectly independent as to all internal affairs and forms of government, will bind all civilized nations in one bond of peace and good-will.

It is no good reason why there should be no Congress of Nations, because it cannot do every thing. Nor will the refusal of one or even many nations to concur, entirely defeat our enterprise. If no other than Great Britain, France and the United States should agree on any article of international law, the principle, thus settled by the three chief commercial powers in the world, would soon become the law of nations, by the bare power and impulse of moral truth. For instance, should these three powers repudiate the practice of privateering,

* John Q. Adams's Phi Beta Kappa Address.   † Micah 4: 3.

the relinquishment of that practice would forthwith be a blessing to the high contracting parties, and this relic of barbarism would soon be relinquished by every Christian nation.

As the contemplated Congress would have nothing to do, and *could* have nothing to do, with the internal affairs of nations, it could be no more dangerous to our free institutions than a treaty of peace and commerce, entered into by us with the ambassador of a monarchical government. Even a general treaty of peace, entered into by all the powers of Christendom, especially if we should not be bound by any article of such a treaty, unless we should voluntarily and formally assent to it, could not endanger our free institutions. Despotic institutions would be more endangered by a Congress of Nations, than our republican principles. It was well observed in the Report of the Committee of Foreign Relations on this subject, presented to Congress at its last session, "War has ever been the fruitful source of arbitrary power. They are, to a certain degree, inseparable." By preventing war, then, we promote free institutions in other countries, and secure them in our own.

If a good thing be liable to abuse, we should not deem that a sufficient argument against its adoption; otherwise we must throw away all the improvements of society, both physical and moral. The constantly advancing improvements in the world are a sure guaranty, that when a thing is good in itself, the good will gain an increasing preponderance, which will finally reduce the evil to the "small dust of the balance." If bodies armed with physical * 174 force are dangerous, it does not follow * that similar bodies, armed only with moral power, will be dangerous also. Bodies so constituted that there is "no appeal from them but to the sword," * may be dangerous, while those that have no appeal but to public opinion may be, at least, harmless. If the fact, that civil war is more bitter than foreign, and that the "battles are more sanguinary, and victory less merciful," * which grow out of the organization of society, be of sufficient weight to discourage such organizations, then society must revert to its first elements, and all government but that of brute force be superseded. Mankind have so long been used to consider the sword as the only legitimate sceptre, by which the world should or could be governed, they forget that there is any power in enlightened public opinion.

"A reference to a third power of all such controversies as could be safely confided to any tribunal unknown to the constitution of our country," has been already recommended by the Committee on Foreign Relations. The Executive of the country has already shown its concurrence by frequently submitting disputes between the United States and other nations to the crowned heads of Europe. This course has received the decided approbation of our own country, and elicited the admiration of the whole Christian and civilized world. The only questions, then, which remain, are these:

1. Whether this course should continue to be an occasional measure, or become a systematic and general rule?

2. Whether the judges, or umpires, in these cases are to act by the immediate

* Mr. Legare's Report on this subject to the last session of Congress.

impression of truth or error on their minds, or be governed in their decisions by known and acknowledged principles and laws, recognized and adopted by the parties in controversy?

3. Whether we should continue to leave our disputes to the monarchs of Europe, singly and individually, or to a body of jurists, selected from the different states composing the proposed confederation, already distinguished for their legal talents and integrity.

On these three topics, your petitioners would briefly remark:

1. Though an occasional reference to a third power is good, a settled and regulated practice is far better, and much more likely to result in the peace and happiness of mankind. Were there a regular and acknowledged tribunal, always ready to judge the cases brought before it, governments would be compelled, by their own constituents, and by the opinion of the world, to resort to it, rather than to the expensive, barbarous, and uncertain decision of the sword. If the antagonist party should refuse to comply, he would find but little sympathy * 175 for * the disasters which might befall him in the course of the war, and be glad to make peace by the intervention of such a tribunal.

2. Such is the infirmity of human nature, such its liability to be influenced by selfish motives, that every possible guard should be provided against errors of judgment arising from such causes. Now, a code of international laws, settled upon abstract principles, before the occurrence of any case to warp the judgment of the framers of such laws, adopted by the compact and agreement of the nations generally, especially, if the contending nations should happen to be parties to the compact, would add greatly to the probability of a just decision by the proposed Court of Nations.

3. It appears almost an anomaly that the United States, "the only republic in the world," * should continue to leave its disputes with other powers to monarchs, who are busy with their own affairs, and who may have difficulties of their own to be settled by the mediation of our opponent. Such was the fact in the case of our north-east boundary question. Ought we not to prefer a tribunal composed of men free from the cares of state, the intrigues of courts, and controversies of their own with other nations; men with an established reputation, knowing that the peaceful execution of their sentence depends not only on the correctness of their judgment, but on their power to make it appear just to the world; that on their ability to make and vindicate a correct decision, depends their present and future reputation? The Governor of the State of Maine told one of your petitioners, that he is morally certain, that if the north-east boundary question had been left to such a tribunal as we contemplate, the case would long ago have been settled to the entire satisfaction of this country.

If "judges do more than pronounce and enforce judgment in particular cases," if "those opinions are the basis of all government and legislation," as is conceded by the author of the very able report already alluded to, how very superior must be a bench of able jurists, of acknowledged talents and integrity,

* Mr. Legare's Report.

to individual umpires, chosen rather for their station than their talents, and liable to have their judgment warped by a thousand extraneous circumstances.

Recent events afford a good opportunity of showing the excellency of the plan proposed by your petitioners. France claims from Mexico an indemnity of about $700,000. Mexico denies the justice of the claim, and refuses to pay. France blockades her ports, and shuts out all other nations from their accustomed commerce. England complains of the blockade as an infringement *176 on her rights, and argues that * France has no right thus to injure Mexico, and through her, all other commercial powers, until she has inflicted a still greater injury on Mexico, by seizing her commerce, and declaring war. Then, it is contended, France would have a right to capture neutral vessels trading to Mexican ports. Now, were there a Court of Nations, France and Mexico would have submitted the case to it, rather than experience so great inconvenience for so small a sum; and had there been a code of international laws, the right of France to blockade, or of neutral nations to trade to, the ports of Mexico, would have been clearly defined. For want of these, war may commence between France and Mexico, and extend to Great Britain and all the commercial world.

The General Court of Massachusetts, one of the most numerous and enlightened legislative bodies in the world, has had this subject under consideration for five years past. At first, the plan was treated as the phantasy of a benevolent enthusiast. Discussion threw light upon it. Resolves recommending a Congress of Nations to the attention of our National Executive, and " to the Legislatures of the several States, inviting their expression of sentiment and cooperation in favor of the end in view," passed the Senate of that State in the year 1837, by a majority of nearly six to one. Last year, similar resolves passed both branches of the Legislature of that State, with only two dissenting voices. The American Peace Society waited for that joyful consummation, ere they ventured to bring this subject before the collected wisdom of the nation. But the New York Peace Society has anticipated us, and the subject has received from your honorable bodies a more kind and respectful attention than they had expected on its first presentation. When the Congress of the Union shall have given the subject as continued and mature deliberation as the General Court of Massachusetts, probably the same results will follow.

Were our contemplated plan to involve great expense, we might, perhaps, pause before we presented it to the consideration of Congress; but the share of expense, falling on this country, would not maintain a single gun-boat. One ship of the line would cost more than a Congress and Court of Nations for the whole civilized world. We should soon be a thousand times repaid by the money saved in the preparation for war; and our agriculturists, merchants, manufacturers and fishermen would reap golden harvests from the increasing wealth of their customers.

If this enterprise would endanger our free institutions, we ought to pause and reflect before we run the hazard even for so great a good; but we are persuaded, that the long-continued peace, which must be the consequence of

* 177 the establishment of an international tribunal, * would not only save our republic from its greatest danger, but, under God, it would be the means of extending the principles of Christianity and freedom all over the world.

The bare attempt, even if it failed, would be glorious. It would show to the world our desire for the peace and happiness of mankind. But the attempt would not fail, if it were persevered in, so as to be distinctly seen and understood by the people of Europe. If only France and Great Britain joined us at first, success would be certain. The work has already begun in England. France will follow. God has destined this country to take the lead in this great enterprise. Let us not be unmindful of our high destiny.

From the abovementioned considerations, and many more which could be urged, your petitioners humbly pray, that your honorable bodies would take such action in the premises, as, after mature deliberation, shall appear best adapted to the end proposed.

WILLIAM LADD, *President.*

J. P. BLANCHARD,	JOHN OWEN,	
H. WARE, JR.,	JAMES K. WHIPPLE,	*Executive*
AMASA WALKER,	EDWARD NOYES,	*Committee.*
GEO. C. BECKWITH,	HOWARD MALCOM,	
L. T. STODDARD,		

No. 10.

Second Petition of the New York Peace Society.

To the honorable, the Senate and House of Representatives of the United States of America, in Congress assembled on the first Monday in December, 1838:— The undersigned, members of the New York Peace Society, and others friendly to the peace cause, respectfully present the following Petition and Memorial:

Your petitioners pray your honorable body to interpose your good offices as mediator between France and Mexico, thereby preventing, if possible, the effusion of human blood, and the great and innumerable evils of war, which, without some interposition of the kind, are almost sure to be realized from the present relative position of those nations.

"Two nations," says Vattel, in his Law of Nations, "though equally * 178 weary of war, often continue it merely from the fear of making the * first advances to an accommodation, as these might be imputed to weakness; or, they persist in it from animosity, and against their real interests. *Then,* common friends effectually interpose, offering themselves for mediators. And there cannot be a more beneficent office, than that of reconciling two nations at war, and thus putting a stop to the effusion of human blood. This is an indispensable duty to those who are possessed of the means of succeeding in it." Now, the present attitude assumed by France and Mexico in relation to each other, presents a fair case for interposition of the kind. It is hardly to be expected, that, in the present stage of the difficulty between those powers, either party will make advances towards reconciliation. Mediation, therefore, is imperatively demanded in this instance, by the interests of human nature. And who so suitable for this office in the case before us, as the government of the United States?—a country that has not only herself repeatedly received the benefit of the friendly interposition of others in a similar way, but that, on the one hand, sees her ancient ally, and, on the other, a sister republic of our own hemisphere, arrayed in fearful hostility against each other.

Your petitioners further pray your honorable body to act as mediator in general, in all cases of international difficulty that now exist between other nations, or that may hereafter occur, while the relations of nations remain in their present state, and no *system* of international arbitration shall be established.

The propriety, the praiseworthiness, the necessity, and the duty, of international mediation in general, are admitted on all hands. "A nation or sovereign," says Vattel, "ought to promote peace as much as lies within their power; to dissuade others from breaking it without necessity; to exhort them to a love of justice, equity, and the public tranquillity, and to a love of peace. It is one of the best offices we can perform to nations, and to the whole universe. What a glorious and amiable appellation is that of peace-maker! The most glorious period of Augustus's life was, when he shut the temple of Janus, adjusted the disputes of kings and nations, and gave peace to the universe." Now, above all others, it is incumbent on these United States to be always ready to promote the welfare of nations. Do not we profess, more emphatically than others, the desire to see all nations in the enjoyment of freedom, and every imaginable blessing? High time, indeed, then, is it, that we ceased to look with apparent unconcern on the sanguinary conflicts of nations, while monarchical governments step in between the contending parties, as ministers of mercy and peace.

Your petitioners still further pray your honorable body, to adopt for * 179 * this government the principle of international arbitration, in reference to all cases of dispute between the United States and other powers, which cannot be amicably adjusted by the parties themselves. The adoption of this principle by your honorable body would follow as a legitimate consequence, from the character which you would assume in acting as peace-maker among the nations. And, moreover, as the propriety of this principle has been repeatedly recognized by this government, by the actual reference of disputes in various instances, this furnishes an additional reason why your honorable body should make it a fixed rule of action.

Your memorialists feel that a few words are requisite in relation to this point; for, though arbitration is occasionally resorted to by nations, war as a custom nevertheless continues.

First, then, it is observable, that war pays no regard to the merits of a case. Its rule is *might*, not *right*. But arbitration *does* consider those merits. Again; the stronger party being more likely than the weaker to be the aggressor, a resort to war in the case renders it probable that the injured party will receive additional injury, instead of obtaining redress; whereas, by arbitration, that party would in all probability *obtain* redress. In cases where two parties are nearly equal in strength, by resorting to war, they generally leave off where they begin, nothing being decided, and both parties being sadly injured. Arbitration in *such* cases, also, would answer a better purpose in both respects. And in cases where the stronger party is the injured one, although by a resort to war, redress is generally obtained, how hard *the way* of obtaining it! Arbitration would afford it in an easier way. In every case, then, the ends of justice are better subserved by arbitration than by war, and all the evils of war are prevented besides. Furthermore; war is an infringement of the independence of nations. Surely it is such an infringement, for one nation to dictate to another, and to attempt to enforce its dictation, as is always done by one of the parties in war. But arbitration respects national sovereignty. Here is no dictation, no coercion, nothing but friendly counsel. Once more; by resorting to war, nations violate one of the plainest dictates of reason, viz., that parties should not be judges in their own cases, which they always assume to be in war. Arbitration respects this dictate, by providing a disinterested party as a judge. Then again; the custom of war affords the strong an opportunity to oppress the weak, and the ambitious to pursue their schemes of conquest and aggrandizement. Arbitration is a check to oppression and ambition, and the best security of the defenceless.

And again; the custom of war, by which nations take their position on * 180 what they denominate the point of honor, refusing * to make the proper concessions and overtures for the preservation of peace, and sacrificing justice itself to resentment and pride, is one vast system of duelling. The principle of international arbitration is the principle of order and peace on a scale of equal magnitude. In short, every reason that can be urged in favor of the peaceful adjustment of individual disputes, and against a resort to individual violence, can be urged with as much greater force in favor of international arbitration, and against war, as the evils of war exceed in every respect the evils resulting from individual combat. Now, then, if the ends of justice itself can be better subserved by arbitration than by war, and so much evil be prevented, and so much good done, what plea remains for war?

Your petitioners yet further pray, that your honorable body propose to the various governments of the world, to appoint suitable persons as delegates, to assemble in congress or convention with delegates from the United States, for the purpose of preparing a code of international law, obligatory on such nations as may subsequently adopt it, and of acting as a board of arbitration, or a court of equity and honor, in cases of dispute between nations which may from time to time be submitted to their consideration.

The present law of nations, so called, is in a very unsettled condition. Many of its principles are matters of dispute, the writers on international law disagreeing among themselves. Nor have they any official authority, even did they agree. Neither is it competent for any one government to regulate the matter. Hence, an international tribunal is the only resource that remains, to set these things in order, and to furnish nations with a suitable code of international law. We say *international* law, because we do not propose that the contemplated tribunal shall interfere with the *internal* concerns of nations. We only say, that some common tribunal is necessary, to lay down general and definite rules for the observance of nations in their intercourse with one another. Should these rules contain any thing objectionable, any nation could refuse to adopt that objectionable part. This conservative principle would be a sufficient guard against encroachment on national rights, and would tend to the production of an equitable code on the part of the tribunal. Should some nations eventually refuse to ratify it, this would not render it abortive; for those nations that *would* ratify it could make it *their* rule in their intercourse with *one another*, leaving things as they now are in relation to the non-concurring powers, till they might see fit to adopt it.

If it is indispensable to society, that civil law be expressed in the form of a code, how great the necessity of having an international code. "The law *181 of nations," says Vattel, "is as much above the civil * law in its importance, as the proceedings of nations and sovereigns surpass in their consequences those of private persons." How plain, how explicit, then, ought the law of nations to be! How guarded at every point! How fixed and acknowledged its principles! And yet, strange to say, this law, all-important as it is, has never, as yet, so much as been put into the form of a code, and many of its principles themselves remain matters of dispute, and have been the frequent occasion of war!

That a nation, under the existing state of things, has sometimes acted in opposition to the general sentiment, and disregarded rules which others have thought proper to observe, is so far from being an argument against embodying international law in a code, that it is the very reverse. A disputed principle of international law is not an established part of it; hence the necessity of having its principles settled, and the admitted law of nations explicitly expressed and recognized. But as the matter now stands, any nation may disregard what *others* choose to consider the law of nations. For, under what obligation is an independent nation to regard the opinions of unauthorized writers on the duties of nations, or to make the practice of other nations an example for itself?

But do your memorialists, in proposing the formation of a code of international law, necessarily involve the idea of innovation upon the established usages and the acknowledged principles of nations? By no means. The present law of nations could be thrown into the form of a code, without a single alteration; and that code, duly recognized by the nations, would be binding. Here would be a definite and certain rule; and even this would be a desideratum. But your memorialists would have, *if practicable*, some improvement made in its *principles*. They would at least have an *attempt* made to improve them. They would have suitable delegates from the various nations *convene*, and discuss and investigate principles, and *see* if they could not agree upon some improvement; and if they could not do this, then let them explicitly state the principles on which they might agree, and this would form a definite code. Some who have no confidence in the utility of a code of the kind, admit that "it could scarcely do any harm." Inasmuch, therefore, as a trial of the experiment could safely be made, why should it not be done, and thus afford the opportunity of bringing its supposed advantages to the test? And the more especially so, when, as they admit, "the authority of law, once established and acknowledged among men, is second only to that of religion." Certainly, if this is so, incalculable good would result from a wise code of international law, enacted by an authorized tribunal, and ratified by the nations themselves.

* 182   * The propriety of the principle of international arbitration being admitted, your memorialists have only to show, that the *mode* of arbitration which they propose is the preferable one. And they are at a loss to perceive how any one, after due consideration, can fail to see, that a council composed of the statesmen, the sages, the philanthropists, the master-minds of earth, having nought to divide their attention, and acting in accordance with a well-digested code, would be as much superior to a temporary, individual arbitrator, looking uncounteracted to his own interest, burthened with the affairs of state, and having to form a decision under the disadvantage of unsettled principles of international law, as can well be conceived.

The establishment of *a system* of international arbitration, and of a Congress of Nations, as proposed by your memorialists, would likewise have great advantages over mere temporary arbitration in other respects. Let it be the understanding, that nations are uniformly to refer their disputes, and let there be a tribunal established to which to refer them, and the various powers would then feel safe in making a great reduction of their naval and military forces, and arbitration would be resorted to without waiting for war to commence. Whereas, without any such system and organization, arbitration being only occasional, it is seldom resorted to till after the commencement of hostilities, and then but occasionally, just as chance or caprice may happen to direct. Under such circumstances, peace cannot be insured, governments will not feel safe in reducing their forces, and thus will the war-system continue. Who, then, can fail to give the preference to the *mode* of arbitration proposed by your memorialists?

Some who object to such a board of arbitrators say, that the probability is, that its decrees "would be merely nugatory." But why nugatory? In cases of ordinary arbitration, decisions in general are not nugatory, though no compulsion is used. Why, then, would the decisions of the contemplated tribunal be nugatory? Should this, however, be the result, no harm would be done, to say the least. That something, nay, that much, *would* be accomplished, is evident from the consideration, that "judges not only pass judgment in particular cases, but shape the opinions of mankind in analogous ones;" and that "those opinions are the basis of all government and legislation."

But then it is feared, that if it *did* have any influence, that influence would be "perverted to the worst ends." Your memorialists are at a loss to perceive how this would be possible. The tribunal under consideration would only be called upon to decide cases of *external* dispute between nations, not those involving principles of government, or any vital principles whatever; in short, nothing

that would be calculated to call into exercise the monarchical or the repub-
* 183 lican sympathies of any * of its members—nothing that a monarchy and a
democracy would hesitate to submit to the arbitration of a crowned head
of a kingdom, or an uncrowned head of a republic. Who dreams of submitting
to arbitration, whether a nation shall have a monarchical or a republican form
of government, or surrender its independence, or be interfered with in any manner
whatever, where others are not concerned? Certainly, not your memorialists!
They merely propose, that such points as are proper subjects for international
arbitration, be referred to a tribunal of the kind already designated, instead of
a temporary, individual arbitrator, or the sword. Where the danger in this? the
more especially, as the parties would only be bound *in honor* to regard decisions
manifestly just. This provision would tend to the production of righteous decisions on the part of the tribunal, inasmuch as unrighteous ones, under such
circumstances, would effect nothing but the disgrace of that body itself. With
far greater propriety, therefore, might the plea of danger be made, in submitting
the disputes of individuals to courts of justice, whereby they are *compelled* to
regard decisions, than in this case of nations. The decisions of the proposed
tribunal would evidently have all the efficacy they ought to have, and no more.
They would have only a moral influence, and that just in proportion to their
rectitude. Thus, while national *independence* would remain inviolate, the ful-
filment of national *obligation* would be secured.

Your memorialists are not a little surprised, that the project of Henry IV
should be seriously compared with the plan by them recommended, and be pronounced far superior in point of practical wisdom. Whether a scheme to revolution-
ize all Christendom; to subjugate and partition the dominant power of the day;
to change the boundaries of states, and apply to them the leveling principle of
agrarianism; thereby interfering with the sovereignty and other primary rights
of nations, and introducing innovations and changes without number; is more
evincive of practical wisdom, than a proposition to draw out the law of nations
into the form of a code, and to reduce the present practice of nations with regard
to arbitration to an orderly system, as proposed by your memorialists, is for
your honorable body to decide.

Nor less are your memorialists surprised, that it should be asserted, that the
famous Amphictyonic Council " had no effect whatever in healing the dissensions
of the Grecian commonwealths." In relation to this Council, Rees says, " Their
determinations were received with the greatest veneration, and were even held
sacred and inviolable." Rollin says, " The authority of the Amphictyons had
always been of great weight in Greece; but it began to decline exceedingly, from
the moment they condescended to admit Philip of Macedon into their body."

Just as your memorialists would have it. A case more to their
* 184 * purpose could not be conceived. The decisions of that Council were
efficacious exactly in proportion to their equity; and they lost their influence when the Macedonian began to pervert it.

The assertion, that the Germanic Diet accomplished nothing for the pacification
of the states of Germany, is equally at variance with history. For three

APPENDIX

hundred years, the German empire had been the theatre of barbarism and anarchy; when Maximilian I accomplished what his predecessors had so long attempted in vain. "In 1495," says the Encyclopædia Americana, "he had put an end to the internal troubles and violence, by the perpetual peace of the empire, decreed by the Diet of Worms."

Your memorialists would here bring into view the auspicious results emanating from the system of arbitration adopted by the Helvetic Union. "The Swiss," says Vattel, "have had the precaution, in all their alliances among themselves, and even in those they have contracted with the neighboring powers, to agree beforehand on the manner in which their disputes were to be submitted to arbitrators, in case they could not adjust them in an amicable manner. This wise precaution has not a little contributed to maintain the Helvetic republic in that flourishing state which secures its liberty, and renders it respectable throughout Europe." The same writer, in allusion to international arbitration, &c., says, "In order to put in practice any of these methods, it is necessary to speak with each other, and to confer together. Conferences and congresses are then a way of reconciliation which the law of nature recommends to nations, as proper to put an amicable period to their differences." Thus is the idea of a Congress of Nations sanctioned by the *law* of nations. Not only so: the *practice* of nations sanctions it. From 1644, to 1814, there were more than thirty convocations of temporary Congresses of Nations, embracing various states of Europe. "Wars have been terminated by them; conflicting jurisdictions have been settled; boundaries have been ascertained; commercial conventions have been formed; and, in various ways, the interests of friendly intercourse have been promoted." Your memorialists, therefore, in proposing the establishment of a Congress of Nations, are far from acting the part of visionary innovators; they merely propose an *improvement* of a present international regulation. They propose, that, instead of temporary congresses, convened after war *has done* its bloody work, there be a permanent Congress to *prevent* war—a body of sages and philanthropists always ready, to whom to refer disputes *before* war, rather than *after* it. This is the sum of the whole matter. And what is there visionary or impracticable in it? What is there in it that is not decidedly better than the present state of things? This * 185 improvement in international jurisprudence, this * advance upon preceding ages, is due from this very generation to the enlightened period in which we live. Your memorialists can but think, that the venerable Franklin had some such plan in view when he said, "We daily make great improvements in *natural*, there is one I wish to see in *moral*, philosophy; the discovery of a plan that would induce and oblige nations to settle their disputes without first cutting one another's throats." Something of the kind the illustrious Jefferson seems likewise to have had in view, when, in speaking of the inefficiency of war in redressing wrong, and of its multiplying, instead of indemnifying, losses, he exclaims, "These truths are palpable, and must, in the progress of time, have their influence on the minds and conduct of nations!" And in authorizing his name to be registered among the names of the members of the Massachusetts Peace Society, he gave still stronger testimony in favor of pacific principles and measures.

Before coming to a close, your memorialists would introduce to the notice of your honorable body what will no doubt, ere-long, be presented in an official form; relating as it does, directly to the subject now under consideration, and having a most important bearing on it.

The Legislature of the noble and enlightened State of Massachusetts have recently adopted a report, and sundry resolutions of a committee of that body, by a unanimous vote in the House, and with only five dissenting votes in the Senate, and consequently without distinction of sect or party, in which they entirely coincide with your memorialists in their views.

[As this part of the memorial, consisting of extracts from the abovementioned report, and the resolutions appended to it, has appeared in a previous article, it is unnecessary to repeat it.]

Thus, not only your memorialists, but virtually whole States, already call on your honorable body to adopt the system of pacification designated in this memorial. Nay, your memorialists doubt not, that could the universal sentiment be ascertained, nine-tenths of the human race would be found to accord with these views. Your memorialists, therefore, present this document to your honorable body, as the representation of the views and wishes of their race, in regard to this great subject; and in the name of human nature they implore you to grant these requests.

Your memorialists fear they have already trespassed on the patience of your honorable body, by their very extended remarks. They trust, however, that the immense importance of the subject will serve as a sufficient excuse for the great length of this memorial. And they only further hope, that your honorable body will give it attention according to that importance. Should this be the case, they are under no apprehensions with regard to the result. And your memorialists, as in duty bound, will ever pray.

No. 11.

* 186   * *Third Petition of the American Peace Society.*

To the Honorable Senate and House of Representatives of the United States of America, in Congress assembled, 1839-40.

The undersigned, President and Executive Committee of the American Peace Society, by the authority, and in behalf of that Society, present the following petition:

Your petitioners, being more persuaded than ever, that the frequency of war may be lessened, its sufferings abated, and the custom of war finally banished from the community of free and enlightened nations, and a more equitable, safe and cheap method for settling international disputes substituted in its place, would once more call the attention of your honorable bodies to that most important subject,—a Congress of Nations. They have nothing to add to the unanswerable arguments of former petitions on this subject, and they lament that the short duration of the last session of Congress prevented the Committee on Foreign Affairs, to whom their own, and many other petitions on the subject were referred, from making a report on the answer of your petitioners, and others from different parts of the Union, to the objections to this great and benevolent enterprise, which were brought against it by the report of the Committee on Foreign Affairs of the preceding session of Congress. The Committee were probably so much occupied with the many important topics brought before them during the short session of Congress, that they had not time thoroughly to examine the subject. If they had examined it, they probably would have come to the same result with the Legislature of Massachusetts, who two years ago almost unanimously recommended the subject to the attention of Congress, by a report and resolves sent on last year to the President of the United States, which want of time probably prevented him from laying before Congress.

The question of our north-eastern boundary is still unsettled and is likely to remain so for years to come; and may bring on a war between two of the most enlightened nations in the world,—a war, which so far from settling the question, would only encumber it with new difficulties to be settled by another umpire, whose decision would be as liable to be rejected as the last; and thus it may continue to be the bone of contention between the two countries, until they see the futility of expecting an individual, however learned and discriminating, to settle a question which may require the united wisdom of a whole bench of judges, long used to weigh conflicting evidences in the scales of justice; and, from * 187 their exalted situation, elevated above all national and * political feelings, able not only to give a right decision, but to make that decision plain and satisfactory to the parties concerned, and to the world at large. The opinion has been expressed by some of the ex-governors of the State of Maine, that had such a Court of Nations as that which we contemplate existed, the difficulties of our north-eastern boundary would long ago have been settled to our entire satisfaction.

The plan proposed by your petitioners is two-fold. One part consists of a Congress of Ambassadors from all those Christian and civilized nations who may choose to be represented there, for the purpose of settling such points of the law of nations, as they may be able to agree upon, in a mutual treaty between all the powers represented, which, like any other treaty, might be ratified or rejected by the nations concerned. The other part is the organization, by that Congress, of a Court of Nations for the adjustment of such cases of international difficulties as might be brought before it by the mutual consent of any two or more conflicting nations, without resort to arms. This is the outline of our plan. The details may be filled up by the wisdom of the present and succeeding ages. The whole plan may be adopted, or either part of it; for one is not *necessarily* dependent on the other. They may exist separately, or both together, as should be thought best. But the two great objects should never be lost sight of, viz., 1st. The settlement of the principles of international law by compact and agreement after mature deliberation; leaving them no longer to be decided by the conflicting opinions of unauthorized writers on the law of nations. 2d. Some better method than the sword, or occasional arbitration, for the settlement of the disputes of Christian and civilized nations; such as a high Court composed of the most celebrated civilians and jurisconsults of the countries represented in a Congress of Nations. The plan is so simple, and the evils to be remedied so great, that the only difficulty seems to be in making men believe that so great a cure can be performed by such simple means, which, after all, is but a step or two in the increasing practice of arbitrating international difficulties.

This subject has been much discussed in New England and New York; and, where best understood, it is most appreciated. It has also received the attention of the British public, and has been agitated on the continent of Europe. Should the government of these United States invite Great Britain and France to join in this great and benevolent enterprise, and these three powers only should commence the work, most of the other powers of Europe and the South American republics would soon follow; and a new era would dawn on the world: right would take the place of might; wars, in a great measure, would cease in Christendom; and peace and happiness would generally pervade the world.

* 188   * The American Peace Society is not alone in this affair, as is abundantly testified by the numerous petitions presented to the last two sessions of Congress on this subject, not only by peace societies, but by men who are not members of any peace society, but who desire the happiness of their fellow-creatures, and the honor and prosperity of their country; and we expect that numerous petitions will be presented to Congress at their present session, if our fellow-citizens have not become discouraged by the neglect of their petitions last winter; for almost every one who understands the subject, readily gives his assent to it.

Deeply impressed with these views of the subject, your petitioners humbly pray that their petition may be committed to a special Committee, with directions to examine and report on the subject.

WILLIAM LADD, *President.*

J. P. BLANCHARD,	JOHN OWEN,	} *Executive Committee.*
GEO. C. BECKWITH,	J. W. PARKER,	
EDWARD NOYES,	JAMES K. WHIPPLE,	

No. 12.

Form of a Petition written and circulated by the Friends of Peace in different parts of the country.

To the Honorable the Senate and House of Representatives of the United States of America, in Congress assembled:

The undersigned, citizens of [Portsmouth, in the State of New Hampshire,] respectfully present the following Memorial and Petition:

It is a growing sentiment among men of all classes and professions, that international war is as needless as it is confessed to be ruinous to the resources and morals of a people. This opinion is now defended, not, as formerly, on religious grounds solely, and by the members of individual sects of Christians, but on grounds of general expediency and policy, and by many who view or treat the subject only in its political aspects. But with this progress of public sentiment, recent events have shown us that the causes of war are not removed; but our country was, during the last year, brought alarmingly near a state of hostility with the very power with which, of all others, a common parentage and language, and the closest financial and commercial relations, invite us to cultivate a pacific intercourse.

* 189   * The most fruitful causes of war flow from the unsettled state of international law. The existence of international law is recognized, and its requisitions are professedly held as binding by all the civilized governments of Europe and America.

International law, in its original growth, has been justly compared to the common law of England and of most of these United States. It has no recognized code; but is the creature of precedent, and individual opinion and authority. It is, therefore, like the common law, ever in the process of creation. Of the latter, it has been said, with truth, that " the courts make it, instead of being governed by it." And so may it be said of international law, that, while it is ostensibly the basis of all diplomatic intercourse, the nations make it by every new demand, compromise or treaty. A system of law, thus perpetually *in transitu*, must, of necessity, be indefinite, and liable to opposing constructions. Moreover, there must necessarily be, both within nations and between nations, however strict and thorough the statuary provisions, a common law, a law of precedent and authority, perpetually growing up. No codification can be so complete as to cover all possible cases, and to cut off the call for independent precedents and decisions.

Yet it seems to your petitioners a self-evident proposition, that a common law may, at a certain stage of its growth, have reached such a degree of complexity, and may have become so voluminous or miscellaneous in its authorities, as to demand codification, and also that it may become established (or capable of being established by a careful comparison of precedents) on a sufficient range of questions and subjects, to render such codification of the greatest value and advantage. To codify such a system of law, is not to arrest it in its progress towards completeness, but to facilitate its progress by writing its history.

This stage, it is believed by many eminent jurists, has been reached by the common law, so called; and much has been of late wisely said and written with regard to its codification. Already in the State of Massachusetts is a commission, composed of gentlemen of the highest legal talents and attainments, engaged, under an act of the Legislature, in the codification of the common law. Nor do we deem it a merely fortuitous coincidence, but the result of analogous views and arguments, that the Legislature of that same enlightened State should have been, so far as we are informed, the first legislative body in the world to recommend by vote " the institution of a Congress of Nations for the purpose of framing a code of international law."

Your petitioners believe that the law of nations is capable of being definitely settled on many points, on which it is still unsettled, and that *190 * the good of the civilized world demands its early establishment and codification, so far as practicable. We reflect with alarm on the admitted fact, that the points of international law, on which opposing views led to our last war with Great Britain, still remain unsettled, and may involve us anew in hostilities with any future belligerent European power. We believe that the present interval of peace and amicable relations between the great powers of Christendom generally, would be eminently favorable to the prospective settlement of the possible grounds of future discord and hostility. We cannot but think, too, that the same disposition, which has led the principal powers of Europe, in repeated recent instances, to adjust, by amicable negotiations, or by arbitration, disputes which, a quarter of a century ago, would have inevitably issued in sanguinary wars, would induce them to accede to any proposal, emanating from a source entitled to the highest regard and deference, for the establishment of a code of international law.

It is mainly in this view that we petition your honorable body to take into mature consideration the subject of a " Congress of Nations." We would respectfully submit the question, whether it be not practicable for a body of accredited delegates from the civilized governments of Europe and America to be convened for the establishment of certain leading points of international rights, usage and intercourse. In proposing such a measure, and urging its practicability, we do not propose and urge an unprecedented measure, or one which requires any unwonted form of negotiation, in order for it to be carried into effect. We are, perhaps, unfortunate, in having given to this, our favorite measure, a new name. There have often been three or more parties to an international treaty; and such treaties have always been negotiated by a " Congress of Nations," that is, by a convention composed of the accredited representatives of the several high contracting powers. Moreover, individual points of international law constitute a part or the whole of the subject matter of every treaty between two or more nations; and by every treaty, such points are settled for a season between the parties to the treaty. The measure, in behalf of which we yet hope to see the influence of our government exerted, is the negotiation of a treaty, to which there shall be as many parties as there are civilized and Christian governments, and which shall embrace all the points of international law which accumulated precedent and authority furnish the means of establishing to general satisfaction.

We look forward to the establishment of a system or law of arbitration for the settlement of future international disputes, as an ulterior result of * 191 the convening of such a " Congress of Nations," as would be * held for the purpose aforesaid. What that system or mode of adjustment would probably be—whether by the renewal from time to time with judicial functions of the Congress originally convened for legislative purposes (to which we are well aware that there are sound and weighty objections), or by defining, by general treaty, the rights, powers and duties of umpires of the respective parties to an arbitration—we do not presume to say. When we urge upon our legislators and others the project of a Congress of Nations, we include this object of the settlement of national disputes with the more definite one of the establishment of a code of international law; because the latter object is of course only auxiliary to the former, and because the latter must needs follow from any train of measures designed to carry the former into effect.

In petitioning your honorable body to take this subject into consideration, we are by no means unaware of the respectful attention paid by the last Congress to similar petitions, or insensible to the merits of the able and candid report presented to the House of Representatives June 13, 1838, by Mr. Legare, from the Committee on Foreign Affairs. We are encouraged still to petition by the very fact, that former petitions have not been presented in vain, but have called great and good minds into action upon a subject of so vital an interest.

We respectfully hope that ours and similar petitions may be the means of drawing out other minds on the same field of inquiry and argument; and also of chronicling on the records of Congress the progress, which we are well assured that the general mind of the American people has made since the presentation of the report just referred to, and which therefore its collective wisdom must indicate.

No. 13.

Petition to Parliament by the London Peace Society.

The humble Petition of the Executive Committee of the Society for the Promotion of Permanent and Universal Peace,

SHOWETH,—That a Society for the promotion of Permanent and Universal Peace was formed in London, in the year one thousand eight hundred and sixteen. That this Society has attempted to effect this end, by diffusing information on the subject, showing that the resort to war, to settle questions of national profit and honor, is a practice derived from the barbarism of former ages; inconsistent
* 192 with the * enlightened philanthropy of the present times; altogether contrary to the benign principles of Christianity; productive of extensive destruction of property, liberty, and human life, and of many other great miseries and corruptions: and usually inefficient for the purposes for which it is waged; and hence, that it is incumbent on all civilized, especially on all Christian communities, to devise measures for its complete suppression.

Your petitioners further show, that societies have been formed in the United States of America, in France, and in Switzerland, for the same purpose, which aim at this most desirable consummation, by precisely the same measures.

Your petitioners take this opportunity to state, that they have been strongly urged, by the American Peace Society, in consequence of the dispute now existing, in reference to the boundary line between the United States and the British territories, to unite with them in endeavoring to allay all angry passions and excited feelings, on a subject which ought to be decided by sound judgment and calm deliberation: and to use all constitutional means to prevent the outbreaking of war between two countries, bound together by so many ties of principle, affection, and interest.

Under a serious apprehension of the danger of a catastrophe so awful, your petitioners earnestly invite the calm consideration of your honorable House, to the principles of the acknowledged religion of this country, and to those petitions in the liturgy of the Established Church of this nation, which pray for the preservation of Peace; and they implore your honorable House to use all efforts which your wisdom may devise, to prevent a calamity so greatly to be deprecated, as a war between two nations of one blood, of one language, and of one religion.

Your petitioners beg leave to express their firm conviction, that all war is opposed to the spirit and precepts of Christianity, and is contrary to the true interests of nations; and that the time is come for the adoption of a more equitable and Christian method of settling international disputes.

Your petitioners therefore humbly pray your honorable House to devise such measures as in its wisdom may seem best adapted, to induce all governments to unite in forming a great council, for the purpose of settling the principles of international law and of organizing a High Court of Appeal, in which all national disputes may be adjusted.

And your petitioners will ever pray.